DRINKS WITHOUT ALCOHOL

DRINKS

Non-alcoholic Slurpies & Smoothies, Cocktails & Punches,

WITHOUT

200 Fresh, Fast & Fruity Little Sips & Great Big Gulps!

ALCOHOL

JANE BRANDT

Illustrations by Robin Zingone

WORKMAN PUBLISHING/NEW YORK

For my children and my grandchildren—Kate, Lauren,
Mike, James, Forrest, Gracie, and both Roberts.

With special thanks and appreciation to
Suzanne Rafer and Katherine Ness,
who patiently and diligently edited these comments and recipes
to assure the best degree of perfection possible.

Copyright © 1983 (as *Drinks Without Liquor*), 1999 by Jane Brandt
All rights reserved. No portion of this book may be reproduced—mechanically, electronically, or by any other means,
including photocopying—without written permission of the publisher. Published simultaneously in Canada
by Thomas Allen & Son, Inc.

Brandt, Jane
Drinks without alcohol: for bashes, beaches, bbqs & birthdays / by Jane Brandt;
illustrations by Robin Zingone—2nd ed.
p. cm.
ISBN 0-7611-1573-0
1. Beverages. 2. Title.
TX815.B83 1999
641.8'75—dc21   99-30062
CIP

Cover and book design by Janet Vicario
Cover and book illustrations by Robin Zingone

Workman books are available at special discounts when purchased in bulk for premiums and sales promotions
as well as for fund-raising or educational use. Special editions or book excerpts can be created to specification.
For details, contact the Special Sales Director at the address below.

Workman Publishing Company, Inc.
708 Broadway
New York, NY 10003-9555
www.workmanweb.com

Manufactured in the United States of America
First printing May 1999
10 9 8 7 6 5 4 3 2 1

CONTENTS

TO YOUR HEALTH

When I first wrote *Drinks Without Liquor* in the early 1980s, the demand for nonalcoholic potables at dinner parties, holiday get-togethers, weddings, bar mitzvahs, and other large social gatherings was fairly small. Those who didn't want a glass of wine or a cup of punch spiked with a little something made do with plain or fizzy water or with a soda. Now, there's nothing wrong with those drinks, but there are so many other enjoyable ways to stir up festive concoctions, it seemed a shame to limit the choices to the old standbys. So the idea for this book was born.

The original collection in *Drinks* invited readers into a world of creative alternatives to alcoholic beverages—and not just for party occasions. The drinks were for all ages and for all times of the day.

Much has changed since the first edition was published. The community of fresh juice aficionados and smoothie lovers is huge. Non-alcoholic punches and cocktails are on the menu at most festive occasions. And coffee has certainly undergone a major face-lift. There are so many marvelous and inviting versions to try, it's a lucky thing they come in decaf as well as caffeinated! With all the attention these beverages were getting, it was time to take another look at *Drinks.* I'm happy to say that the original selection is as solid now as it was almost twenty years ago. The fruity slushes and citrus ades, the vegetable energizers, the sweet punches and flavored coffees, all are timely and terrific. The book also offers a luscious selection of ice cream sodas and shakes—and here's where time has worked in our favor. The last couple of decades have brought us delicious low- and nonfat alternatives to whole milk and super-rich ice cream, rescuing those of us who are concerned about calories and fat content. Use these new choices to create the ice cream parlor concoctions that are included here. On a day when you need to give yourself a special sweet treat, nothing tastes better than a good old-fashioned ice cream (or frozen yogurt) soda.

Besides the updated favorites, you'll find a sampling of new recipes, including vitamin-packed fruit and vegetable juicer drinks, such as the glamorous Orchid Isle, and some more smoothies (try Midge's Mudslide for an indulgent low-fat dessert).

When I first wrote this book, I was raising six children. Today I boast of eight grandchildren and am still involved in the business world. And I still find that, busy or not, it's great fun to be able to offer these special drinks to my family and friends. I know you'll enjoy them too.

So, Skål, Cheers, Bottoms Up, L'Chaim, Down the Hatch, To Your Health, and Here's Looking at You, Kid. Toast in the New Year and continue throughout the seasons with this festive array. Besides those yummy shakes and ice cream floats, there are sweet and fruity energizers to pick you up after a hectic morning, flavorful vegetable cocktails to serve before an elegant dinner, and enough creative concoctions to keep your party punch bowl popular.

Included too are low-calorie quenchers for the diet conscious, a whole slew of warming broths for cold winter days, and children's favorites for birthday celebrations, get-togethers, and sleepovers.

When unexpected family or friends drop in, when special party occasions arise, or when someone just wants something good to drink, *Drinks Without Alcohol* is ready to inspire you.

ICE

Ice blocks and rings melt slower than cubes, and they're especially good for those large-crowd punches.

◆ To make a plain ice block, simply use a container large enough to suit your need: plastic storage boxes are useful, or you can use a cake pan, an angel-food pan, a loaf pan, or even a mixing bowl for an extra-large block. Use ring or other shaped molds to add interest.

◆ To color an ice block or ring—for a St. Patrick's Day party or Valentine's Day brunch—just add food coloring to the water before freezing.

◆ To make it really festive, decorate the ice block, mold, or individual cubes: fill the container halfway with water and freeze it. Remove the container from the freezer, and arrange your decorations on the ice: unsprayed flowers and greens; fresh herbs and fresh fruit; even mini American flags for the Fourth of July. Then carefully add ½ inch of water and refreeze. When the decoration is set, fill the container the rest of the way, and freeze it thoroughly.

◆ To unmold an ice block or ring, dip the container briefly in a bowl of hot water. Slide the ice carefully into your punch bowl. If possible, put the ice in the bowl before you add the punch to avoid overflows. If the punch is already in the bowl, go slowly!

◆ When crushing ice, never place whole cubes in your blender unless your instruction booklet says it's okay. If you aren't sure, put the cubes in a plastic bag first, then whack them with a mallet or hammer to break them into smaller pieces. Now add them to the blender to complete the crushing.

USING THE RECIPES

I have given sugar quantities in these drinks according to my family's taste, but of course you may wish to adjust them to your own. If you like less sugar, try cutting the amount in half, and then add to it until the drink tastes right to you.

◆ In recipes that call for large quantities to be put through a blender, I have divided the amount into two batches to avoid any disastrous overflow. If in doubt, or if your blender is particularly small, you can always do the mixing in even smaller batches.

◆ Where punch cups are indicated, I've calculated 5-ounce servings.

◆ In punches that have sherbet and soda as ingredients, you may find that a while after blending, the milky solids float to the top and the soda remains on the bottom. Just be sure you stir the punch a bit as you ladle it out.

◆ As I mentioned earlier, you may substitute a favorite low- or nonfat ice cream or frozen yogurt in any of the recipes calling for ice cream.

MORNING MEDLEYS

A checkered tablecloth, sunshine bouncing off a bouquet of garden flowers, orange juice or cantaloupe cocktails in sparking goblets or old-fashioned glasses, cinnamon buns warm from the oven . . . and over all the aroma of freshly brewed coffee beckoning your guests to celebrate a new day—this is the morning medley.

Breakfasts and brunches are wonderful occasions for entertaining. Your energy level is high, and if you use your imagination you can put together an unforgettable buffet. But don't serve these rise-and-shine winners only to guests. As a special treat, surprise your own family one morning with a small bowl of punch along with the pancakes, and watch it empty before your eyes.

BREAKFAST SMOOTHIE

A blender breakfast for the calorie-conscious, this smoothie is like the very best fruit salad in a glass.

> 1 cup plain low-fat
>   yogurt
> ½ cup honey
> ½ cup sliced fresh
>   strawberries
> ½ cup diced ripe papaya
> ½ cup diced ripe cantaloupe
> 3 tablespoons raw sugar
> 2 tablespoons wheat germ
> 1 cup crushed ice
> Cantaloupe slices, for garnish

1. Place half of the yogurt, honey, fruit, sugar, and wheat germ in a blender and blend on medium speed until smooth, 30 seconds. Pour into a pitcher.

2. Place the other half of the ingredients in the blender and add the crushed ice. Blend on high until smooth, 1 minute.

3. Add the iced mixture to the rest, stir well, and pour into frosted glasses. Garnish with the melon slices.

SERVINGS: 4 GLASSES

POWDER POWER

Probably no food has received more accolades of late than the soy bean. High in protein and low in fat, soy is thought to be helpful in fighting everything from heart disease to cancer to menopausal symptoms. Until fairly recently you had to eat a lot of tofu to reap any soy benefits, but now there are much easier ways to get soy into your diet. One of the easiest and most readily available is soy protein powder, and there's no better food to blend it into than a tasty breakfast smoothie. So if soy is your thing, add a spoonful of powder to you favorite fruit combination and bottoms up!

CANTALOUPE COCKTAIL

A country breakfast table is the perfect spot for launching these appetizing morning cocktails. But it will be just as welcome in a city apartment, as long as the melon is ripe and juicy.

Flesh of 1 medium-size ripe cantaloupe,
*   diced*
3 tablespoons lime juice,
*   preferably fresh*
2 cups orange juice, preferably fresh
2 tablespoons sugar
¼ teaspoon vanilla extract
Pinch of salt
Wafer-thin lime slices, for garnish

1. Place all the ingredients, through the salt, in a blender and blend on low speed until smooth, 20 seconds.

2. Serve in frosted old-fashioned glasses, garnished with a lime slice.

SERVINGS: 6 OLD-FASHIONED GLASSES

FRUITY FLING

The next time friends spend a summer weekend at your house, wake them up with this. For the fullest flavor, chill the juices first.

1 quart orange juice, preferably fresh
1 cup grapefruit juice, preferably fresh
1 cup pineapple juice
1 pint raspberry sherbet
Orange zest or maraschino cherries,
*   for garnish*

Mix the juices in a large pitcher and pour over cracked ice in tall glasses. Add a scoop of raspberry sherbet, top with orange zest or a cherry, and put a straw and long-handled spoon in each glass.

SERVINGS: 6 TALL GLASSES

DELUXE ORANGE JUICE

A velvety smooth and delicately colored juice drink. It is frothy and fancy—natural and invigorating.

> 1 cup fresh orange juice
>   (2 oranges)
> ¼ cup bottled lime juice
> Confectioners' sugar, to taste
> 1 egg white
> 3 ice cubes
> Wafer-thin orange or
>   lime slices, for garnish

1. Place all the ingredients, through the egg white, in a blender and blend on medium speed for 10 seconds.

2. Add the ice cubes and blend on medium speed until well mixed and frothy, 1 minute.

3. Pour into glasses and garnish with orange or lime slices.

SERVINGS: 2 SMALL GLASSES

ORANGE JUICE

Oranges are available in the supermarkets all year round and can be quite inexpensive when purchased in quantity. Sliced thin, they are always a colorful garnish for fruit-based or tea drinks. They can also be scooped clean of pulp and used as containers for fruit granités (see page 64). But we almost always think of oranges in terms of orange juice, perhaps the most popular morning juice—a delicious and refreshing way to start the day, as well as a ready source of energy.

NUMBER OF ORANGES (MEDIUM-SIZE)	QUANTITY OF JUICE
1	½ cup
4	2 cups
8	4 cups
20	10 cups

LONG BEACH ISLAND TALL BOY

This is a terrific breakfast or brunch eye-opener. There's plenty of bright citrus flavor, just the right thing first thing in the morning.

> 1 can (6 ounces) frozen lemonade
>   concentrate, thawed
> 1 quart orange juice,
>   preferably fresh
> Strawberries and wafer-thin
>   lime slices, for garnish

1. Prepare the lemonade in a large pitcher according to the instructions.

2. Add the orange juice and stir well.

3. Pour into frosted glasses filled with ice, and add a strawberry and a lime slice to each.

SERVINGS: 8 LARGE JUICE GLASSES

A JUICE LOOSENER

To get more juice from lemons, limes, and oranges:

Squeeze the fruit when it is at room temperature. If it's still cold from the refrigerator, warm the fruit slightly in a container of hot tap water.

Or, before squeezing, roll the fruit back and forth on the counter surface, pressing hard with your palm. This softens the pulp.

JANIE'S JUICE JUBILEE

If the thought of a big breakfast makes you gag, drop these ingredients into your juicer and start the day "vitamized" and "energized." It's a favorite of my daughter, Jane.

1 ripe banana
1 Valencia or navel orange
1 apple, such as
    McIntosh, Winesap,
    or Delicious
1 ripe Bartlett
    pear

1. Peel and quarter the banana.

2. Peel and section the orange.

3. Rinse, quarter, and core the apple and pear.

4. Put all the fruit through a juicer. Stir and serve.

SERVINGS: 1 TALL GLASS

THE PICK-UP MAN

At a rodeo, the most skilled riders are the "pick-up men," who literally pick up the tired, dusty cowboys, pulling them out of the path of the wild bulls and bucking broncos. This juicer drink is guaranteed to pick *you* up and put you back in the saddle.

2 Valencia or navel oranges
½ fresh pineapple
1 McIntosh or Delicious apple
1 pint fresh strawberries

1. Peel and quarter the oranges.

2. Peel, quarter, and core the pineapple.

3. Rinse, quarter, and core the apple.

4. Rinse and trim the strawberries.

5. Put all the ingredients through a juicer. Stir and serve.

SERVINGS: 4 SMALL GLASSES

TOMATO FRAPPE

Serve these at breakfast while hungry guests are waiting for those special omelets. Most of the preparation is done 24 hours in advance, so you can concentrate on the eggs.

1 tablespoon butter
3 tablespoons finely chopped
    onion
1 teaspoon sugar
1 tablespoon lemon juice,
    preferably fresh
Generous dash of Worcestershire
    sauce
4 cups tomato juice
Lemon wedges, for garnish

1. Melt the butter in a small skillet over medium-low heat. Add the onion and sauté until golden, about 5 minutes.

2. Place the sautéed onion, sugar, lemon juice, Worcestershire sauce, and tomato juice in a blender. Blend until smooth, 1 minute. Pour into a plastic container, leaving about 1 inch of space at the top. Cover and freeze for about 2 hours.

3. Half an hour before serving, remove the container from the freezer. Break the tomato mixture into chunks with a heavy fork, and blend it, a little at a time, in a blender on low speed just until smooth—don't let it melt. Serve in fancy sherbet glasses with lemon wedges and straws.

SERVINGS: 4 TO 6 SHERBET GLASSES

MULLED TOMATO JUICE

You can make this easily in your crockpot. It will keep the juice hot until serving time. Serve it at an elegant brunch.

2 large cans (46 ounces each)
    tomato juice
1 tablespoon Worcestershire sauce
1 teaspoon celery salt
½ teaspoon dried oregano
8 tablespoons (1 stick) butter,
    at room temperature
Dash of Tabasco sauce
Sprigs of parsley or watercress,
    for garnish

1. Put all the ingredients, through the Tabasco, in a crockpot set on high. Heat for 20 minutes.

2. Ladle into punch cups, garnish with sprigs of parsley or watercress, and serve.

SERVINGS: 24 PUNCH CUPS

CURRIED CLAM AND TOMATO

The combination of clam and curry makes this extra-special for a formal brunch. It can also be served as an appetizer at any meal.

2 cups bottled clam
    juice
1 cup tomato sauce
½ teaspoon curry powder

Place all the ingredients in a blender and blend for 1 minute. Pour over crushed ice in short glasses.

SERVINGS: 6 SMALL GLASSES

Note: You can substitute 1 bottle (16 ounces) Clamato juice for the clam juice and tomato sauce.

PIRATE'S BREATH

A brunch punch that's fast and easy. Your guests will never be able to guess the ingredients. Make it as hot and spicy as the company will allow!

> *2 bottles (32 ounces each) Bloody*
> *Mary mix*
> *2 quarts orange juice*
> *Worcestershire sauce, to taste*
> *Tabasco sauce, to taste*
> *Thin orange slices, for garnish*

1. Combine the Bloody Mary mix and orange juice in a punch bowl, and stir gently.

2. Taste the mixture, and add Worcestershire and Tabasco. Start with a few drops of each, then stir and taste before adding more.

3. Just before serving, put an ice ring (see page 2) in the punch bowl.

4. Garnish the punch with the orange slices.

SERVINGS: 16 MUGS

PINK LADY PUNCH

Another concoction that's great for mid-morning brunch. Sweet, tart, and with just enough fizz.

> *1 quart cranberry juice cocktail*
> *1½ cups sugar*
> *4 cups unsweetened pineapple or grape-*
> *fruit juice*
> *2 quarts ginger ale*

1. Place the cranberry juice, sugar, and pineapple juice in a punch bowl and stir well.

2. Just before serving, add the ginger ale and ice cubes and stir.

SERVINGS: 32 PUNCH CUPS

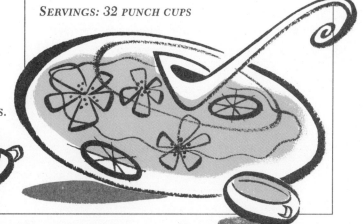

ANNIE'S FANCY

An exceptional punch for a bunch at brunch . . . or any time you have a large thirsty crowd.

>*1 cup fresh orange juice*
>*1 cup prepared lemonade*
>*1 cup prepared limeade*
>*1 cup tangerine juice*
>*1 large can (46 ounces)*
>   *pineapple juice*
>*2 quarts ginger ale, chilled*
>*Wafer-thin orange, lemon, and lime slices,*
>   *for garnish*

1. Place all the juices in a punch bowl and stir well. Refrigerate until you are ready to serve.

2. Just before serving, add the ginger ale and ice cubes and stir. Float the fruit slices on top in the punch bowl.

SERVINGS: 40 PUNCH CUPS

EVEN STEVEN

This is the traditional café au lait: easy to prepare, soothing, and especially nice served in an attractive mug or delicate teacup.

>*2 cups strong hot coffee*
>*2 cups hot milk (not boiling)*

Carefully pour equal amounts of hot coffee and milk *simultaneously* into your coffee cups. Serve piping hot.

SERVINGS: 4 CUPS

HINTS FOR THE PERFECT CUP OF COFFEE

◆ *Contrary to an old wives' tale about dirty coffee pots making the best coffee, the pot should be scrupulously clean. Coffee has a great deal of oil in it, and if it is allowed to accumulate in the pot it will add bitterness to a newly made cup.*

◆ *Regardless of how you brew coffee, a broken eggshell in the pot will absorb much of the bitterness and any impurities in the coffee that might make it murky.*

◆ *Once the can is opened or the beans are ground, coffee loses its flavor quickly. Store it in an airtight container in the refrigerator.*

◆ *Be certain to use the proper grind for the method you are using:*
  Regular grind for percolators
  Drip grind for drip pots and vacuum coffee makers
  Electroperk for electric coffee makers

◆ *Measure coffee carefully; the quantities are the same for all methods.*

◆ *Regardless of which method you choose to brew coffee, after it is made it should never be allowed to boil. Keep it hot by placing the pot on a hot tray or in a pan of hot water over very low heat.*

ORANGE COFFEE

A refreshing midmorning drink, or wonderful at lunchtime, especially when served in a fancy goblet.

1 cup strong coffee, chilled
1 cup cold milk
1 cup orange juice, preferably fresh
2 tablespoons sugar
Orange slices, for garnish

Place all the ingredients, through the sugar, in a blender and blend on medium speed for 1 minute. Pour into frosted glasses, and garnish each with an orange slice.

SERVINGS: 2 LARGE GLASSES

GINGER-PEACHY COFFEE FOR A CROWD

Nothing could be better for an elegant morning brunch than this punch. The aroma alone will entice your guests!

1 cup heavy (whipping) cream
2 cups cold water
3 tablespoons dark brown sugar
½ teaspoon ground cinnamon
¼ teaspoon ground ginger
1 can (10½ ounces) sliced peaches,
    drained (reserve the liquid)
6 cups strong hot coffee
Grated orange zest, for garnish

1. Pour the cream into a bowl and beat with a mixer until whipped. Set aside.

2. In a large saucepan over medium heat, combine the water, brown sugar, cinnamon, ginger, and reserved peach liquid. Allow the mixture to come to a boil; then reduce the heat and simmer for 1 minute.

3. Place the peaches and half the coffee in a blender and blend on high speed until smooth, 1 minute.

4. Add the blender mixture and the rest of the coffee to the saucepan. Stir until well mixed and thoroughly hot.

5. Serve in glass mugs, topped with a dollop of whipped cream and some grated orange zest.

SERVINGS: 12 MUGS

COFFEE MEASUREMENTS FOR ALL GRINDS		
COFFEE (TABLESPOONS)	**WATER (CUPS)**	**SERVINGS**
2	1½	2
4	3	4
6	4½	6
8	6	8
10	7½	10
½ pound	4 quarts	20
1 pound	8 quarts	40
1½ pounds	12 quarts	60

APPLE COFFEE

This is another crowd pleaser—the mulled cider-coffee combination is unusual and a perfect choice to take along on a Sunday drive in the country.

> *1 quart apple juice*
> *1 quart strong hot coffee*
> *6 oranges, scrubbed and sliced*
>   *wafer-thin*
> *3 cinnamon sticks (3 inches each)*
> *⅓ cup dark brown sugar*
> *Pinch of ground allspice*
> *Pinch of ground cloves*

1. Place all the ingredients in a large saucepan and bring to a boil over medium heat. Reduce the heat and simmer for 10 minutes.

2. Remove the saucepan from the heat, and strain the liquid into a pitcher or thermos. Serve in mugs.

SERVINGS: 8 MUGS

PEANUT BUTTER COFFEE

Don't rush to turn the page—this is worth tasting! It makes a surprising and different iced coffee.

> *1 cup strong coffee, chilled*
> *1 cup cold milk*
> *1 heaping tablespoon peanut butter*
> *2 tablespoons sugar*

Place all the ingredients in a blender and blend until smooth, about 2 minutes. Serve over ice in tall glasses.

SERVINGS: 2 TALL GLASSES

MOCHA COFFEE

Serve this either hot or cold, depending on the weather. It is excellent following a meal, or in the morning instead of regular coffee.

> *1 tablespoon powdered instant coffee*
> *1 teaspoon chocolate syrup*
> *1 cup milk, heated to the boiling point, or*
> > *1 cup boiling water and 1 tablespoon*
> > *heavy (whipping)*
> > *cream, or 1 cup cold milk*

HOT: Mix together the instant coffee and syrup in a coffee cup. Add the hot milk, or the boiling water and cream, stir, and serve.

COLD: Place the instant coffee, syrup, and cold milk in a blender and blend until well mixed. Pour into a tall glass over ice.

SERVINGS: 1 CUP

Note: For the cold version, instead of 1 cup milk, try half milk and half cream, or half milk and half club soda.

FANCY CAFE MOCHA

Combine equal quantities of hot chocolate and strong hot coffee. Pour into cups and top with whipped cream. Then sprinkle with grated nutmeg or orange zest.

EASY ESPRESSO

For each serving use 3 ounces of fresh cold water to each coffee measure of Italian roast drip-grind coffee. Prepare in a regular drip pot. Serve in demitasse cups or in wine glasses, with a twist of lemon peel and some sugar cubes for dunking.

INSTANT COFFEE FOR A CROWD

For the midmorning coffee break at, let's say, your club's annual speaker series, have this quick pick-me-up at the ready.

> *1 cup powdered instant coffee*
> *6 quarts cold water*

Combine the instant coffee and water in a large pot. Heat just to boiling and ladle out immediately.

SERVINGS: 32 COFFEE CUPS

THE CZAR'S TODDY

This is a recipe for a dry mix that can be stored in a covered container. It is excellent to keep on hand as an instant beverage to enjoy at home or at the office.

3 cups sugar
2 cups orange-flavored
*   breakfast drink (powdered*
*   concentrate)*
1 cup unsweetened
*   instant tea mix*
1 teaspoon ground
*   cloves*
1 teaspoon ground cinnamon
Large kettle boiling water

1. In a medium-size bowl, combine all the ingredients and mix well. Store in an airtight container.

2. To serve, put 2 rounded tablespoons of mix in each cup. Fill with boiling water and stir well.

SERVINGS: 32 TEACUPS

TEA

The proverbial teapot is a warm way to welcome one guest or many. There are literally hundreds of kinds of tea, and it's fun to have a variety on hand, in loose form or in bags. Since the flavors vary quite a bit—from the delicate Oolong to the smoky Souchong or the many spicy blends that are available—you should experiment to see which appeals to you the most.

Teapot tea is best when preparing more than one cup at a time. It is always good to preheat the pot: simply rinse it with boiling water. Then measure the loose tea into the pot—½ to 1 teaspoon of tea leaves per cup of water, according to the strength you like. Pour in the boiling water. You will see the tea leaves begin to float. Put the cover on the pot and allow it to stand for 3 to 5 minutes—any longer and the tea will acquire a bitter taste. Then pour the tea through a tea strainer into each cup. (Antique silver tea strainers with ornate handles are a lovely addition to a formal tea.)

You can eliminate messy straining by purchasing a tea ball—a small strainer with a screw-on lid that is filled with loose tea and placed directly in the teapot before adding the boiling water. Some teapots come with a built-in strainer.

Whether you are making cold or hot tea, always use a glass, china, or earthenware pot or pitcher. Metal changes the flavor of tea.

COCOA HONEY

For lazing around with the Sunday papers or at bedtime with a good novel.

1 quart milk
1 cinnamon stick (3 inches)
¼ cup powdered cocoa mix
Pinch of salt
¼ cup honey

1. Place the milk and the cinnamon stick in a medium-size saucepan over low heat, and heat just to the boiling point (do not boil). Remove from the heat.

2. Discard the cinnamon stick. Pour ½ cup of the hot milk into a small bowl, and stir in the cocoa and salt.

3. Return the cocoa mixture to the remaining hot milk, place over low heat, and gradually stir in the honey. Serve in warmed mugs.

SERVINGS: 4 MUGS

BORED-WITH-COCOA COCOA

Mmmm! Keep some anise flavoring on hand so you can offer this unusual drink to a special guest on a moment's notice.

3 tablespoons chocolate syrup
1 cup hot milk
1 teaspoon anise flavoring (see Note)

Combine the syrup and hot milk in a cup, and stir in the anise.

SERVINGS: 1 MUG

Note: Anise (licorice) flavoring can be found in bigger supermarkets as well as specialty food stores.

CHOCOLATE DELUXE

For those with discerning taste. Don't forget to pass the butter cookies.

4 egg whites
¾ cup powdered cocoa mix
Pinch of ground cinnamon
½ cup sugar
2 quarts milk
Whipped cream or chocolate shavings,
*   for garnish*

1. Combine the egg whites, cocoa, cinnamon, sugar, and ½ cup of the milk in a blender. Blend on medium speed for 15 seconds.

2. Pour the blender mixture into a large saucepan, and add the rest of the milk. Heat until very hot but not boiling. Pour into pretty teacups and garnish each with whipped cream or chocolate shavings.

SERVINGS: 8 TO 12 TEACUPS

COCOA SUPREME

Ordinary cocoa becomes richer with a little half-and-half.

4 heaping teaspoons
*   powdered cocoa mix*
Pinch of salt
4 teaspoons sugar
1 cup boiling water
3 cups half-and-half,
*   heated*
Marshmallows,
*   for garnish*

1. Combine the cocoa, salt, and sugar in a small bowl.

2. Put 1 teaspoon of the mixture in each mug. Then add ¼ cup boiling water and fill with half-and-half. Stir well, and float a marshmallow on top.

SERVINGS: 4 MUGS

ANTIDOTES FOR SPRING FEVER

Chase away spring fever with an energizing pick-me-up. Yogurt is just what the blender orders, easily combined with fresh fruit for what can only be described as a heavenly and, best of all, nonfattening drink.

Spring is also a time for family celebrations. Mothers and fathers have special days; Easter dinner awaits. Brides and grooms, showers for the mother-to-be, graduations, and class reunions are all on the horizon and need an original and delicious beverage to accompany traditional cakes and treats.

Open the window wide and welcome the return of the warm weather!

THE PRETTY MOMMA

Just looking at this healthful combination of pineapple and apricot makes you feel good—and the taste is divine. If you find a good ripe pineapple, use it to make this drink (see Note).

1 can (20 ounces) crushed
pineapple
1 cup apricot nectar
1 quart light cream
or half-and-half
⅓ cup sugar
1 teaspoon grenadine syrup
Pineapple cubes, for garnish

Place half of each ingredient, through the grenadine syrup, in a blender and blend on medium speed until smooth, 30 seconds. Pour into 3 frosted glasses and garnish with some of the pineapple cubes. Repeat with the remainder of the ingredients.

Servings: 6 tall glasses

Note: To make this drink with a fresh ripe pineapple, first cut off the top leaves from the fruit. Quarter the pineapple and remove the center core and peel from each piece.

Cut the flesh into small cubes, and set some aside for garnish. Place the remainder in the blender and process until smooth. Remove half the pineapple purée and set aside. Then proceed with the recipe.

PINEAPPLE CARROT COCKTAIL

Low in calories, high in nutrition, and it goes especially well with a cottage cheese salad or chunks of tofu seasoned to taste with garlic oil, balsamic vinegar, and freshly ground pepper.

3 cups unsweetened pineapple juice
2 large carrots, cut into small pieces
½ teaspoon lemon juice, preferably fresh
1 cup crushed ice

1. Place the pineapple juice, carrot pieces, and lemon juice in a blender and blend until liquefied.

2. Add the crushed ice and blend again, until the ice is liquefied. Stir well.

3. Serve immediately.

SERVINGS: 6 OLD-FASHIONED GLASSES

CHILLY JILLY

Trying to lose weight and thirsty for something tart? Rev up that juicer!

1 tangelo or navel
orange
1 lemon
1 lime
Low-sodium seltzer
Artificial sweetener, to taste,
or 1 tablespoon honey (optional)

1. Peel the orange, and scrub the lemon and lime.

2. Cut the fruit into 1-inch pieces and put through the juicer.

3. Pour the juice into a glass and top with seltzer. Stir in artificial sweetener or honey, if desired.

SERVINGS: 1 GLASS

BILLY BOY'S APRICOT-YOGURT SMOOTHIE

An energizing pick-me-up, or perfect for a springtime breakfast eye-opener.

3 cups chopped, drained canned
*   apricots*
¼ cup apricot preserves
4 cups plain low-fat yogurt
Cold milk as needed
Wheat germ, for garnish

1. Place the apricots and preserves in a food processor or blender and process until puréed, about 2 minutes. Pour the purée into a bowl.

2. Add the yogurt to the purée, beating with a wire whisk until fully incorporated.

3. Add just enough milk to the mixture to thin it slightly, but not too much or you'll lose the tangy apricot flavor. Refrigerate, covered, for about 1 hour.

4. Serve in mugs with a sprinkling of wheat germ on top.

SERVINGS: 6 MUGS

CUPBOARD KEEPERS:
. . . JUST ADD PINEAPPLE JUICE

Pineapple juice can be used with a variety of other juices and sodas to make a quick and thirst-quenching drink. Add equal parts of one of the following:

Papaya juice

Ginger ale, 7-Up, or club soda

Orange juice

Apricot juice

Strong tea (cold)

Cranberry juice cocktail

THE SPORTSMAN

A high-protein milkshake, the perfect pick-me-up at any time of the day—or night. If you prefer, try 1 teaspoon maple syrup, frozen orange juice concentrate, or any fruit nectar in place of the molasses.

1 cup cold milk
1 teaspoon powdered
*   brewer's yeast*
2 tablespoons (or more) powdered
*   skim milk*
1 teaspoon molasses

Place all the ingredients in a blender and blend on medium speed until smooth, 1 minute. Serve immediately.

SERVINGS: 1 MUG

ORCHID ISLE

A sensational orchid-colored beverage from your juicer, perfect for an intimate lunch for two.

1 pint blueberries
2 cups red seedless grapes
3 McIntosh or Delicious apples

1. Rinse the fruit, removing all stems from the berries and grapes.

2. Rinse, quarter, and core the apples.

3. Put all the ingredients through a juicer. Stir, and serve.

SERVINGS: 2 GLASSES

HOT CELERY PICK-ME-UP

A nutritious substitute for lunch, and a definite change of pace for the calorie-counter. Perfect for a raw spring day.

2 quarts beef stock, fresh
    or canned
4 to 6 large ribs celery with
    leaves, chopped
1 large carrot, chopped
2 leeks, well cleaned and
    finely chopped
¼ pound very lean
    ground beef
4 egg whites, beaten
    to a froth
½ teaspoon dried thyme
6 whole black peppercorns
¼ teaspoon dried
    tarragon
Salt and freshly ground
    black pepper, to taste
Chopped celery leaves, chives,
    or parsley, for garnish

1. Place the stock in a large saucepan and bring to a boil over medium heat. Add the celery, cover, and simmer for 30 minutes.

2. Put the carrot, leeks, and beef in another large saucepan. Gently stir in the beaten egg whites and the seasonings. Gradually add the hot stock, stirring constantly. Heat, stirring often, just to boiling. Reduce the heat and simmer for 20 minutes.

3. Place a sieve over a large mixing bowl, and gently ladle the mixture into the sieve, pressing the solids with the back of a wooden spoon to extract as much liquid as possible. Set aside to cool for 1 hour.

4. Serve in clear punch cups (or freeze in small containers for future use). Garnish with chopped celery leaves, chives, or parsley.

SERVINGS: 8 PUNCH CUPS

THE GREEN QUEEN

These vegetables are available all year round, so pull out the juicer and enjoy this drinkable salad any time you like.

6 broccoli flowerets (about 2 cups)
1 medium-size cucumber
1 rib celery
1 green bell pepper
1 clove garlic
Juice of ½ lemon

1. Rinse all the vegetables. Stem the bell pepper.

2. Cut the vegetables into 1-inch pieces.

3. Put the vegetables and the garlic through a juicer.

4. Stir, and season with the lemon juice.

SERVINGS: 1 TALL GLASS

Note: For a creamy drink, substitute ½ cup plain low-fat yogurt for the lemon juice. This will give you 2 medium-size servings.

GARNISHES FOR VEGETABLE DRINKS

Parsley	*Scallions*
Watercress	*Chopped chives*
Celery sticks	*Paprika*
Cucumber sticks	*Freshly ground black pepper*
Carrot sticks	
Carrot curls	*Black or green olives*
Cherry tomatoes	*Cocktail onions*

COCONUT MILK COCKTAIL

Only one or two recipes in this book call for fresh coconut milk because grappling with a coconut is hard work. But the reward is worth it. Don't tackle this concoction without an ice pick and a hammer.

1 coconut
Boiled water, cooled to warm
Grated coconut and/or grated nutmeg, for
 garnish

1. Preheat the oven to 300°F.

2. Puncture the eyes of the coconut with an ice pick or a long sharp nail. Drain and reserve the "milk."

3. Place the drained coconut on a baking sheet and bake, whole, for 15 minutes. Then tap the shell with a hammer to open it. Remove the meat from the shell and chop it coarsely.

4. Place equal amounts of coconut meat and warm water in a blender and blend on high speed until evenly ground, 1 minute. Cool. Strain the coconut water through a sieve or cheesecloth into a bowl. Press hard to extract all the liquid. Add the reserved coconut milk. Cover and refrigerate.

5. Pour the coconut into small glasses and sprinkle with grated coconut and/or nutmeg.

SERVINGS: 6 SMALL GLASSES

CAROLYN'S COCONUT CUTIE

Ideal if you have a sweet tooth as well as an eye for energy. The soda lightens the drink while adding a bit of fizz.

½ cup orange juice,
preferably fresh,
chilled
½ cup plain low-fat yogurt
½ cup cream of coconut
¾ cup club soda
2 wafer-thin orange slices,
for garnish

1. Place the orange juice, yogurt, and cream of coconut in a blender and blend on medium speed for 1 minute.

2. Place 1 or 2 ice cubes in 2 tall frosted glasses. Fill the glasses halfway with the mixture, then gently add the club soda. Garnish each glass with an orange slice.

SERVINGS: 2 TALL GLASSES

TED'S A.B.C.

Excellent for a child's lunch box if you want to be sure of good nourishment during school days. Skip the juice pak and fill a thermos with this instead.

3 cans (12 ounces each) apricot nectar,
chilled
2 bananas, sliced very thin
1 cup canned or fresh coconut milk
(see Note)
Shredded coconut, for garnish

Place half of the apricot nectar, bananas, and coconut milk in a blender and blend on high speed until smooth, 1 minute. Pour the mixture into a bowl or pitcher, and repeat with the other half of the ingredients. Stir the batches together and serve in frosted mugs with shredded coconut sprinkled on top.

SERVINGS: 6 MUGS

Note: For fresh coconut milk, prepare the Coconut Milk Cocktail on the facing page without the garnish.

SPINSTER'S POSSET

Way back in the 15th century, a posset was a substitute meal for invalids or people with sensitive stomachs. In olden days the milk was already warm because it came straight from the cow. Although it's usually made with a bit of wine in order to curdle the milk, I have substituted a good "nip" of lemon juice.

1 quart milk
2 tablespoons fresh lemon juice
    (save the rind)
4 ounces sugar cubes
½ teaspoon ground ginger
½ teaspoon grated nutmeg
Grated nutmeg, for garnish

1. Heat the milk in a large saucepan to just below boiling. Add the lemon juice (the milk will curdle slightly), and remove from the heat.

2. Line a sieve with cheesecloth, place it over a medium-size bowl, and strain the milk through the sieve.

3. Rub the sugar cubes on the lemon rind.

4. Add the sugar cubes, ginger, and nutmeg to the milk. Stir until the sugar dissolves.

5. Pour into punch cups, garnish with extra nutmeg, and serve hot.

SERVINGS: 6 TEACUPS

SASSY STOMACH?

When your tummy's acting up, help it out by making Ellen's Energizer. For 1 tall glass you'll need:

½ cup half-and-half
½ cup ginger ale

Pour the half-and-half over crushed ice in a tall glass. Add the ginger ale slowly, stirring constantly.

THE FARMER'S DAUGHTER

If you can't get fresh buttermilk, you can make the equivalent amount using powdered buttermilk concentrate, which can be found in most supermarkets.

1 quart buttermilk
1 pint lemon sherbet, softened
1 teaspoon sugar
Pinch of ground cinnamon

1. Place the buttermilk and sherbet in a mixing bowl and whisk until smooth.

2. Pour into tall frosted glasses, and sprinkle each with a little sugar and cinnamon.

SERVINGS: 4 TALL GLASSES

RAINBOW BUTTERMILK

Pick a color for this nutritious drink, or make one of each— pink, lavender, yellow. (For individual drinks, use 1 cup of buttermilk to ½ cup of juice).

3 cups buttermilk
1½ cups fruit juice (cherry, apricot, pineapple, peach, or grape)
1 tablespoon sugar, or to taste
Grapes and fruit slices, for garnish

1. Mix all the ingredients, through the sugar, in a pitcher, and stir until the sugar dissolves.

2. Place several grapes in the bottom of each punch cup. Add the drink, and top with a fruit slice.

SERVINGS: 6 TO 8 PUNCH CUPS

ENERGY INNOVATION

Delicious even if you already feel energetic.

1 cup cold milk
½ cup vanilla low-fat yogurt
1 package (10 ounces) frozen raspberries,
*   thawed*
1 egg (see Note this page)

Place all the ingredients in a blender and blend on medium speed until smooth, 1 minute. Serve in tall glasses.

SERVINGS: 2 TALL GLASSES

HOW TO SEPARATE AN EGG

Gently crack the shell by rapping it on the edge of a bowl or cup, making sure the yolk doesn't break. Keep the yolk in one half of the shell and allow the white to run out into the bowl. Carefully transfer the yolk from one half to the other several times, until all the white has drained into the bowl.

THE PRAIRIE OYSTER

For the strong at heart:
You swallow the egg yolk whole!
(And it's guaranteed to cure a hangover.)

1 very fresh egg yolk, or 1 whole egg
*   (see Note)*
1 teaspoon Worcestershire sauce
2 dashes white vinegar
2 dashes Tabasco sauce
Pinch of salt
Freshly ground black pepper, to taste

Place the unbroken egg yolk (or whole egg) in a champagne glass and add the remaining ingredients. Then, down the hatch—good luck!

SERVINGS: 1 GLASS

Note: To avoid any risk of salmonella, eggs must be fresh and uncracked. They must also be continuously refrigerated. Buy your eggs at a market where there is a rapid turnover and where they're kept well chilled.

THINK THIN COFFEE MILKSHAKE

No one will ever guess that this scrumptious shake contains only 85 calories.

1 cup cold skim milk
3 ice cubes, crushed
1 teaspoon powdered instant coffee
Artificial sweetener, to taste

Place all the ingredients in a blender and blend until creamy.

SERVINGS: 1 TALL GLASS

COFFEESCOTCH

Eight delicious servings of a chilled coffee with a rich flavor that will long be remembered by your guests. Serve this cold for dessert, accompanied by plain butter cookies or biscotti.

1 cup butterscotch topping
¾ cup heavy (whipping) cream
5 cups strong coffee, chilled
1 pint coffee ice cream, softened
Grated nutmeg, for garnish

1. Place half of each of the ingredients, through the ice cream, in a blender and blend on medium speed until smooth, 30 seconds. Pour the mixture into a pitcher and repeat with the second half of the ingredients.

2. Serve in tall glasses or coffee mugs, garnished with a grating of nutmeg.

SERVINGS: 8 TALL GLASSES

THE FRITZER

This sophisticated cocktail is something like a spritzer— but not quite!

1 sugar cube, or 1 teaspoon sugar
2 dashes bitters (see Note)
Strip of lemon or orange zest
Club soda

Place the sugar in an old-fashioned glass and add the bitters, zest, and 2 or 3 ice cubes. Fill with club soda and stir.

SERVINGS: 1 OLD-FASHIONED GLASS

Note: You can find bitters—a liquid flavoring used in drinks and other foods—in most supermarkets. Angostura is the most common brand.

GUATEMALAN BEAN BOOSTER

A fully nourishing juicer drink taken from a Guatemalan diet staple—black bean salad.

1 can (15 ounces) black beans
1 small can (8 ounces) corn kernels
1 carrot
1 large, ripe tomato
1 small cucumber
1 clove garlic
Cayenne pepper, to taste
White vinegar, to taste

1. Drain and rinse the black beans and corn.

2. Rinse the carrot, tomato, and cucumber, and cut into 1-inch pieces.

3. Put all the ingredients through a juicer.

4. Season the juice with vinegar and cayenne pepper to taste, and serve.

SERVINGS: 2 SMALL GLASSES

SAUERKRAUT JUICE COCKTAIL

Those of us who love the taste of sauerkraut enjoy sipping this pungent cocktail.

1 cup sauerkraut juice
Pinch of onion powder
Juice of ½ lemon

Thoroughly mix all the ingredients together and pour over crushed ice.

SERVINGS: 1 COCKTAIL GLASS

THE ORAM

An exasperating drink for someone with a sweet tooth, but perfect for those who crave the unusual. This goes well with fresh Brie and other cheese appetizers.

2 cups tomato juice
2 cups sauerkraut juice
Strips of lemon zest
Tabasco sauce (optional)

Place the tomato and sauerkraut juices in a pitcher and stir well. Serve over crushed ice in cocktail glasses, adding a strip of lemon zest to each glass and, if you dare, a dash of Tabasco.

SERVINGS: 8 COCKTAIL GLASSES

THE RUGBY

This one is not for the faint of taste buds. It's a rough-and-tumble power-packed energizer—a great juicer creation. As rugby fans say, "Good Ruck!"

½ cup parsley
2 cups (tightly packed)
fresh spinach leaves
1 tomato
4 carrots
1 rib celery
1 slice (½ inch thick) fresh ginger
1 clove garlic
Pinch of cayenne pepper (optional)
1 teaspoon prepared horseradish
(optional)

1. Thoroughly rinse the vegetables. Trim them and cut into 1-inch pieces.

2. Put the vegetables, ginger, and garlic through a juicer.

3. Stir, and season with a pinch of cayenne pepper and the horseradish (if you dare).

SERVINGS: 2 SMALL GLASSES

THINK AND DRINK HEALTHY

"An apple a day keeps the doctor away"—age-old words of wisdom. Or how about these: "Eat those carrots—they're good for your eyes," "Bread crusts will curl your hair," and last but not least, "Spinach will make you strong." My wonderful mother raised my brother and me with these and other axioms, encouraging us to be members of the "clean plate club."

For generations, parents have known instinctively that fruits and vegetables are good for their kids. Now the medical profession has documented that the juice form of fresh fruit and vegetables is one of the best direct sources of many vitamins and minerals—for people of all ages. Juicers can be purchased in most cookware, department, and chain stores. They are priced for all budgets. You can also find a number of books and manuals that address specific health conditions and the nutrient values of juices; they are available in bookstores and libraries as well as health food stores.

Note: Always peel oranges and grapefruit before putting them through a juicer; the skin contains a mildly toxic substance. Kiwi, papaya, and mangos grown in foreign countries should also be peeled first (the fertilizer used may contain carcinogens). Apple seeds should not be juiced.

COLOR IT RED

A delicious appetizer or light luncheon drink. Bring out the juicer for this one—but keep the white linens in the closet!

½ head red cabbage
1 medium-size beet
1 thin slice onion
1 rib celery

1. Cut the cabbage into small pieces.

2. Rinse and peel the beet, and chop it into small pieces.

3. Rinse the celery, and cut it into 1-inch pieces.

4. Put all the ingredients through a juicer. Stir, and serve.

SERVINGS: 1 GLASS

SAVORY PIZZA SMOOTHIE

Have a real yen for pizza but don't want the calories? Try this for savory flavor! It's good almost any time of the day.

1 can (8 ounces) tomato juice
1 clove garlic
3 heaping tablespoons low-fat ricotta
*   cheese*
¼ teaspoon Italian seasoning
2 parsley sprigs or fresh basil leaves,
*   for garnish*

1. Place the juice, garlic, ricotta, and Italian seasoning in a blender. Blend on high speed until smooth for 30 seconds.

2. Fill 2 glasses with ice cubes, and divide the shake between them. Garnish with parsley or fresh basil leaves.

SERVINGS: 2 COCKTAIL GLASSES

THE CUKE

Toast the Easter Bunny with this while passing a tray of cut-up raw vegetables. May be made in advance—it gains momentum in the refrigerator.

> 2 cups chopped, seeded, peeled
>   cucumber
> 1 quart buttermilk
> 1 tablespoon finely chopped
>   scallions
> Salt and freshly ground black pepper,
>   to taste
> Pinch of garlic powder
> 1 tablespoon finely chopped
>   fresh parsley
> Wafer-thin cucumber slices
>   (do not peel), carrot curls, and
>   paprika, for garnish

1. Place half of each of the ingredients, through the parsley, into a blender and blend on high speed until smooth, 1 minute. Pour the mixture into a large pitcher or a bowl, and repeat with the other half of the ingredients.

2. Combine the batches in the pitcher, mix well, and chill in the refrigerator for 2 hours.

3. Serve in punch cups, with a cucumber slice, a carrot curl, and a sprinkling of paprika on top of each one.

SERVINGS: 8 SMALL PUNCH CUPS

CURLING CARROTS

To make carrot curls, use a vegetable peeler to cut thin strips; wrap the strips around your finger and quickly drop them into a bowl of ice water until you're ready to serve. The ice water will hold the curl in place.

TRIPLE ORANGE

Colorful, bright, nutritious, and supremely easy in your juicer. This fruit and veggie cooler will surprise you with its unusual and delightful flavor. If you can find tangelos, use them here; if not, navels make a fine substitute. For a lighter thirst quencher, add seltzer water.

½ cantaloupe
3 carrots
1 tangelo or navel orange

1. Peel the cantaloupe and cut it into 1-inch pieces.

2. Rinse the carrots and cut them into 1-inch pieces.

3. Peel and section the orange.

4. Put all the ingredients through a juicer.

5. Stir, and pour into 2 frosted glasses.

SERVINGS: 2 GLASSES

BUGS BUNNY

This blender drink is delightful with ham salad made from the Easter dinner leftovers. Use skim milk instead of heavy cream and you will also have a zesty low-calorie companion.

1 large carrot, cut into small pieces
1 can (10½ ounces) condensed chicken
*   broth*
2 cups heavy (whipping) cream or skim
*   milk*
½ teaspoon celery salt
½ teaspoon onion salt
Freshly ground black pepper, to taste
Carrot sticks topped with green olives,
*   for garnish*

1. Place all the ingredients, through the pepper, in a blender and blend on high speed until smooth, 1 minute.

2. Pour the mixture into a medium-size saucepan and warm over low heat, stirring constantly.

3. When it is hot, serve immediately in punch cups, with an olive-topped carrot stick for a stirrer in each cup.

SERVINGS: 6 TO 8 PUNCH CUPS

THE MARINER

Put this in a thermos, grab a fishing pole, and head for the dock.

> *1 Valencia or navel orange*
> *2 cups watermelon pieces*
> *1 cup red seedless grapes*
> *1 apple, such as McIntosh, Winesap,*
>   *or Delicious*

1. Peel and quarter the orange.

2. Rinse the grapes and remove the stems.

3. Rinse, quarter, and core the apple.

4. Put all the fruit through a juicer. Stir and serve.

SERVINGS: 2 GLASSES

STRAWBERRY SLIM

A pretty drink with a delicate flavor and a delicate color. It's perfect for any time of the day.

> *2 cups fresh strawberries*
> *½ cup club soda*
> *½ pint vanilla low-fat ice*
>   *cream or frozen yogurt*
>   *or 1 container (8 ounces)*
>   *vanilla low-fat yogurt*
> *½ cup skim milk*
> *Fresh mint leaves, for garnish*

1. Rinse and hull the strawberries.

2. Place all the ingredients, through the milk, in a blender and blend until smooth, 1 minute.

3. Serve garnished with whole mint leaves.

SERVINGS: 4 TALL GLASSES

STRAWBERRY (NOT-SO) ANGEL

This is really a luscious liquid parfait, so don't serve it with a heavy dessert—just some lacy cookies or a few slices of fresh fruit.

1 pint fresh strawberries, rinsed, hulled, and chopped, or 2 cups frozen strawberries and juice, thawed
1 can (13½ ounces) sweetened condensed milk
2 cups crushed ice
Whole strawberries, for garnish

Place all the ingredients, through the ice, in a blender. Blend on high speed until smooth, 1 minute. Serve in punch cups or in tulip champagne glasses, with a strawberry on top.

SERVINGS: 6 PUNCH CUPS

STRAWBERRY PINEAPPLE SHAKER-UPPER

A real showstopper, but not for the scale hopper! Then again, by substituting nonfat frozen yogurt for the ice cream and sherbet, even the calorie-conscious can give this a try.

1 package (10 ounces) frozen strawberries, thawed
1 can (20 ounces) crushed pineapple
1 pint strawberry sherbet
1 pint vanilla ice cream
1 quart club soda
Pineapple chunks, for garnish

1. Place half of the strawberries, pineapple, sherbet, and ice cream in a blender and blend on high speed for 1 minute. Pour into a large bowl. Repeat with the remaining half, and stir the batches together.

2. Fill each glass two-thirds full with the mixture. Then slowly add club soda to the top. Stir and serve, garnished with a pineapple chunk.

SERVINGS: 6 TALL GLASSES

RAMBLING ROSE PUNCH

A refreshing and colorful addition to your Easter buffet table, this will complement a salty ham or a garlicky roast leg of lamb.

4 packages (10 to 12 ounces each) frozen
strawberries, thawed
1 large can (12 ounces) frozen lemonade
concentrate, thawed
Raspberry and mint ice mold (see Note)
2 quarts ginger ale, chilled
Wafer-thin orange slices, for garnish

1. Place the berries and lemonade (undiluted) in a punch bowl and mix well.

2. When you are ready to serve, carefully add the ice mold to the mixture and pour in the ginger ale. Float orange slices on top.

3. Serve immediately.

SERVINGS: 16 TO 20 PUNCH CUPS

Note: See page 2 for information on making festive ice rings and other molds.

SWEET SLUSH

These exciting beverages are easy to prepare once you have the frozen fruit cubes on hand in the freezer.

2 cups frozen fruit cubes
(see Frozen Fruit
Cubes, facing page)
⅓ cup buttermilk or
plain low-fat yogurt
3 teaspoons sugar
Mint sprigs, for garnish

1. Place the frozen fruit cubes in a blender, but don't turn it on. Allow them to soften slightly, about 10 minutes.

2. Then add the buttermilk and sugar and blend on high speed until smooth, 1 minute. Pour into tall glasses and add a sprig of mint to each.

SERVINGS: 2 TALL GLASSES

FROZEN FRUIT CUBES

Prepare frozen peach, strawberry, pineapple, or watermelon cubes by cutting pieces of the fruit into ¾-inch chunks (the fruit should be peeled, seeded, and cored first, if necessary). Dip each chunk into fresh lemon juice and place the cubes on a cookie sheet, not touching. Put the sheet in the freezer. When the fruit cubes are frozen solid (about 2 hours, depending on your freezer), remove them and store them in a freezer bag in the freezer. These can also be used to cool any fruit beverage. They're pretty to look at, and they won't dilute the drink.

SAVORY LIME SLUSH

Use low-calorie ginger ale and sugar substitute, and you'll have a diet cooler.

2 cups frozen fruit cubes
    (see Frozen Fruit Cubes,
    this page)
⅓ cup ginger ale
2 tablespoons fresh lime juice
1 tablespoon sugar
Fresh mint leaves or wafer-thin lime slice,
    for garnish

1. Place the frozen fruit cubes in a blender, but don't turn it on. Allow them to soften slightly, about 10 minutes.

2. Then add the ginger ale, lime juice, and sugar and blend on high speed until the mixture turns to slush, 30 seconds. Pour into a tall glass and garnish with mint leaves or a slice of lime.

SERVINGS: 1 TALL GLASS

FESTIVE PUNCH

A creamy variation of the Rambling Rose Punch, use it to celebrate any springtime occasion.

3 cans (6 ounces each)
frozen lemonade concentrate
1 package (10 ounces)
frozen strawberries,
thawed and drained
1 quart ginger ale, chilled
Ice ring (see page 2)
1 pint raspberry sherbet,
slightly softened
Whole raspberries, for garnish

Prepare the lemonade according to the directions. Pour it into a punch bowl and stir in the strawberries. Just before serving, add the ginger ale and an ice ring. Then stir in the sherbet. Place a raspberry in each cup, and serve the punch.

SERVINGS: 24 PUNCH CUPS

KENTUCKY DERBY

A mock mint julep drink. Make a pitcherful and let the Derby begin.

4 or 5 mint sprigs
1½ cups sugar
2 cups cold water
¾ cup lemon juice, preferably fresh
1½ quarts ginger ale
Wafer-thin lemon slices, for garnish

1. Rinse the mint and remove the leaves; discard the stems.

2. Place the sugar, water, and lemon juice in a medium-size bowl, mix, and then stir in the mint leaves. Allow to stand for 30 minutes.

3. Fill a larger pitcher with ice cubes, and strain the liquid over the ice. Add the ginger ale and lemon slices, and serve.

SERVINGS: 10 TALL GLASSES

THE MINT STINT

Another marvelous, thirst-quenching treat for Derby Day gatherings. Pass the peanuts!

2 cans (6 ounces each) frozen lemonade
concentrate, thawed
5 cups cold water
2 tablespoons finely chopped
fresh mint leaves
Wafer-thin lemon slices and
mint sprigs, for garnish

1. In a large pitcher, combine the lemonade with the water. Stir and add the chopped mint.

2. Fill tall glasses with ice cubes, add a lemon slice and a sprig of mint to each, and fill with the Mint Stint.

SERVINGS: 6 TALL GLASSES

GRAPE SPRITZER

This soothing drink can be made in any quantity. It's nicest served in wine glasses and makes a fine accompaniment to dinner entrées.

1 quart ginger ale, chilled
1 quart unsweetened grape juice,
chilled

Mix the ginger ale and grape juice in a pitcher or decanter, and serve in wine glasses.

SERVINGS: 16 WINE GLASSES

A WORD ABOUT SPRING WATER AND MINERAL WATER

When a recipe calls for water you may, if you wish, substitute a mineral water or a natural sparkling water. Alone, with ice and a twist of lime, these spring waters have distinct flavors, depending upon their origin. They are pure, containing no calories and usually no salt.

If you live in an area where the water is heavily treated, you would definitely want to consider these spring waters to avoid the possibility of a medicinal or chlorine taste in your beverages.

JUNE PUNCH

Grand for any occasion, this punch goes well with tiny sandwiches or desserts and cakes.

6 cups extra-strong tea
2½ cups sugar
3 cups orange juice,
*   preferably fresh*
2 cups unsweetened grapefruit juice
½ cup lime juice, preferably fresh
½ cup lemon juice, preferably fresh
2 quarts ginger ale
Mint sprigs and wafer-thin lemon
*   slices, for garnish*

1. Place all the ingredients, through the lemon juice, in a punch bowl and stir well. Refrigerate until you are ready to serve.

2. Just before serving, add the ginger ale and some ice cubes, and stir.

3. Garnish the punch with mint sprigs and lemon slices.

SERVINGS: 40 PUNCH CUPS

TAILS AND VEILS

A punch all wedding guests will adore. Be sure to have plenty on hand.

1 cup sugar
Juice of 6 lemons, strained
1 cup grenadine syrup
3 large cans (46 ounces each) unsweetened
*   pineapple juice, chilled*
2 quarts ginger ale, chilled
1 quart orange sherbet, slightly softened
Fresh strawberries and orange slices,
*   for garnish*

1. Place the sugar, lemon juice, and grenadine in a large punch bowl and stir to mix well. Add the pineapple juice, stir, and refrigerate until you are ready to serve.

2. Just before serving, remove the punch from the refrigerator, add the ginger ale, and gently stir in the sherbet.

3. Place a strawberry and an orange slice in the bottom of each punch cup, and serve.

SERVINGS: 48 PUNCH CUPS

BRIDAL SWEET

This punch may be made in advance in large quantities. Don't wait for a wedding to serve it; any big party will do.

6 cups water
10 tea bags
3 cups sugar
3 cups orange juice, preferably fresh
3 cups unsweetened pineapple juice
1 cup strained fresh lemon juice
2 quarts ginger ale
Fresh mint leaves, for garnish

1. Bring the water to a boil in a saucepan, add the tea bags, and remove from the heat. Allow to steep for 5 minutes.

2. Discard the tea bags. Add the sugar, stir, and chill for at least 3 hours.

3. Place the chilled tea in a punch bowl, add the juices, and stir.

4. Just before serving, stir in the ginger ale. Add ice cubes and garnish with mint leaves.

SERVINGS: 48 PUNCH CUPS

CINDERELLA'S GLASS SLIPPER

Drink a toast to your new house or new job with this rosy cooler (or if there's a wedding being celebrated, toast the bride and groom).

Sugar lumps (1 for each serving)
Bitters (see Note, page 36)
Fresh strawberries
(a few for each serving)
Lemon twists (1 for each serving)
Ginger ale, chilled

For each serving, put a sugar lump in the bottom of a tulip champagne glass and add a dash of bitters, several fresh strawberries, and a lemon twist. Fill with cold ginger ale.

SERVINGS: 1 AND UP

UNREAL CHAMPAGNE

Here's another delicious way to toast the bride and groom—and it's even pink!

1 cup sugar
2 cups water
2 cups unsweetened grapefruit juice
Juice of 1 lemon, strained
¼ cup grenadine syrup
2 bottles (28 ounces each) ginger ale
Strips of lemon zest, for garnish

1. Combine the sugar and the water in a small saucepan over medium heat and cook, stirring constantly, just until the sugar is dissolved, 1 minute. Remove from the heat and allow to cool.

2. Place the grapefruit juice, lemon juice, and grenadine in a punch bowl. Add the sugar syrup and stir well. Refrigerate until you are ready to serve.

3. Just before serving, add the ginger ale and some ice cubes and stir. Ladle the punch into champagne glasses, adding a strip of lemon zest to each.

SERVINGS: 18 CHAMPAGNE GLASSES

FROSTING GLASSES

Half an hour before serving time, rinse the glasses or mugs in cold water and place them, still wet, in the freezer.

If you like, dip the rim in a saucer of sugar (for fruitades) or salt (for a vegetable drink) to coat it before freezing.

MILK SHRUB PUNCH

Shrubs are old-fashioned fruit-based drinks, but there's nothing dated about this one. The raspberry flavor comes through to make this the award-winning punch for all time.

1 quart cold milk
1 quart raspberry
*   sherbet*
1 quart 7-Up, chilled
1 package (10 ounces)
*   frozen raspberries, thawed and*
*   drained (reserve the juice)*
Fresh mint leaves, for garnish

1. Place the milk and sherbet in a blender in batches, and blend on medium speed until smooth, 30 seconds (see Note).

2. Pour the blender mixture into a punch bowl, and add some ice cubes and the 7-Up. Stir gently.

3. Stir in the raspberry juice. Float the berries on top, and garnish with mint leaves.

SERVINGS: 30 PUNCH CUPS

Note: This punch can be made up to 1½ hours ahead to this point. Pour the mixture into a large plastic container, cover, and place in the coldest part of your refrigerator until serving time. Then continue with the rest of the recipe.

GARNISHES FOR FRUIT AND MILK DRINKS

Mint leaves

Lemon or lime slices

Orange slices

Thinly sliced cantaloupe

Red and green maraschino cherries

Whipped cream

Chocolate whipped cream

Candy canes

Peppermint candies

Jelly beans

Cinnamon sticks

Pineapple chunks (skewered on toothpicks with cherries)

Fresh strawberries

Cranberries

Raspberries

Shaved chocolate

Nutmeg

Shredded coconut

Grapes

Melon balls

Raisins

PEACHY KEEN

Perfect for a baby shower. Toast the mother-to-be with this creamy, exciting pick-me-up. It's best with fresh peaches.

1 cup sliced peeled peaches
(preferably fresh)
1 cup light cream or half-and-half
⅓ teaspoon almond extract
1 pint vanilla ice
cream
2 cups cold milk
Fresh mint leaves, for
garnish

1. Combine the peaches, cream, almond extract, and ice cream in a blender. Blend on high speed until smooth, 1 minute.

2. Pour into a pitcher and stir in the milk.

3. Serve in sugar-rimmed frosted glasses (see page 50), and top each with a mint leaf.

SERVINGS: 4 TALL GLASSES

EXOTIC MANGO TROPICALE

I use mangos from my own tree—one of the benefits of living in Florida—for salads and juicer drinks. They can be added to almost any fruit juice combination with delicious results. If you can't get fresh mangos, substitute bottled mango or papaya juice to taste.

1 mango
½ fresh pineapple
3 kiwis
Shredded coconut, for garnish

1. Peel and pit the mango, and cut it into 1-inch pieces.

2. Peel, quarter, and core the pineapple.

3. Peel the kiwis and quarter them.

4. Put the fruit through a juicer.

5. Stir the juice, pour it into tall goblets, and garnish with shredded coconut.

SERVINGS: 4 GOBLETS

FRUITY PUNCH FOR FIFTY

Nifty and thrifty for weddings, graduations, reunions, and other large gatherings.

3 pounds sugar
4 quarts cold water
2 quarts finely minced pineapple
    (canned or fresh)
1 quart unsweetened grapefruit juice
1 quart lemon juice (made from
    concentrate)
3 quarts orange juice
¼ cup grated lemon zest
¼ cup grated orange zest
1½ tablespoons whole cloves
10 cinnamon sticks (3 inches each)
2 tablespoons ground allspice
4 cups strong hot tea
Wafer-thin lemon slices or Frozen Fruit
    Cubes (see page 45), for garnish

1. Place the sugar and water in a large soup pot. Bring to a boil, reduce the heat, and simmer for 5 minutes. Set aside to cool.

2. Strain the pineapple (reserve the juice for another use) and place it and the fruit juices in a large punch bowl.

Add the lemon and orange zest. Stir in the sugar-water mixture.

3. Put the spices in the hot tea and allow to steep for 15 minutes. Strain into the punch bowl.

4. Just before serving, add an ice block and garnish with lemon slices, or add Frozen Fruit Cubes.

SERVINGS: 50 PUNCH CUPS

BASHES, BBQS, BEACH PARTIES

Summer's arrived and so has a thirst for long, cool drinks. You'll want to be prepared when friends drop by for an informal backyard barbecue, the kids come home from a successful Little League or soccer game, or a neighbor needs a tasty reward after mowing the lawn. Take advantage of all those fabulous summer fruits and vegetables—and remember, there's a whole world beyond plain old iced tea! If the great weather signals a beach day, many of these recipes can be poured into a thermos and carried off to enjoy after a swim.

Keep in mind, too, that ice cream concoctions don't necessarily have to be full fat to be full flavored. By all means substitute your favorite low- or nonfat frozen yogurt in any of the sodas, shakes, and smoothies that call for ice cream.

HALFSHELLS

A zesty appetizer to serve to tired sailors or before the main meal at a clambake.

¼ cup chopped celery
1 small onion, finely chopped
1 teaspoon prepared horseradish
¼ cup ketchup or chili sauce
2 cups bottled clam juice
Wafer-thin lemon slices, for garnish

1. Place the celery, onion, horseradish, and ketchup in a blender and blend on high speed to liquefy, 1 minute.

2. Turn the blender off and slowly add the clam juice. Stir gently.

3. Serve over ice, with a slice of lemon in each glass.

SERVINGS:
4 SMALL GLASSES

ICED COFFEE PARK AVENUE

An exotic taste you will enjoy over and over again, no matter the season.

2 cups strong hot coffee
½ teaspoon bitters (see Note, page 36)
½ teaspoon vanilla extract
1 tablespoon sugar
12 coffee ice cubes (see page 61)
1 quart club soda
Wafer-thin orange slices and maraschino cherries, for garnish

1. Place the coffee, bitters, vanilla, and sugar in a large heat-resistant pitcher. Stir well and allow to cool.

2. Place 2 coffee ice cubes in each of 6 glasses. Divide the coffee mixture equally among the glasses.

3. Fill the glasses to the top with club soda, and garnish each one with an orange slice and a cherry speared on a toothpick.

SERVINGS: 6 TALL GLASSES

SPICY DIET ICED COFFEE

Drink this occasionally if you're counting those little calorie devils, or all summer long if you're just plain thirsty and love the taste of coffee.

3 cups strong hot coffee
1 cinnamon stick (3 inches)
3 whole cloves
½ teaspoon ground allspice
Artificial sweetener, to taste
Strips of orange zest

1. Pour the coffee into a bowl or pitcher and stir in the cinnamon stick, cloves, and allspice. Let it stand for 2 hours.

2. Remove the cinnamon stick and the cloves, and pour the coffee over ice in tall glasses. Add artificial sweetener to taste, and garnish each serving with a strip of orange zest.

SERVINGS: 4 TALL GLASSES

BASIC ICED TEA

This is a quick method for making a delicious iced tea. If you have some on hand, use fresh pineapple cut into spears as stirrers.

2 ounces (about ⅔ cup)
*   loose tea,*
*   or 6 tea bags*
1 quart boiling
*   water*
3 quarts cold water
Sugar, to taste (optional)
Lemon slices, for garnish

1. Place the tea in a teapot and add the boiling water. Stir, and allow to steep for 6 minutes.

2. Place the cold water in a punch bowl with ice. Strain the concentrated tea into the cold water and stir. Add sugar to taste.

3. Serve with lemon slices, and place a stirrer in each glass.

SERVINGS: 20 GLASSES

SOLAR SENSATION

Here's a way to make iced tea in the backyard on one of those hot summer days when you can't bear to heat up the kitchen and you're in no particular rush.

3 quarts cold water
8 tea bags
Sugar, to taste
Fresh lemon juice, to taste
Mint sprigs, for garnish

1. Place the cold water and the tea bags in a large glass pitcher and set it in a spot that will remain sunny most of the day.

2. At dinnertime, remove the tea bags and add sugar and lemon juice to taste (or allow guests to add their own). Serve over ice, with a mint sprig in each glass.

Servings: 12 glasses

SMOOTHIE TO A "TEA"

A creamy twist for iced-tea lovers—a grand companion for a sandwich or a good book.

1 cup double-strength tea, chilled (can be
*   herbal tea)*
½ cup lemon or orange nonfat yogurt
Lemon slices, for garnish

1. Combine the tea and yogurt in a blender and blend for 20 seconds.

2. Pour into chilled mugs, and slip a slice of lemon onto the rim of each mug.

Servings: 2 mugs

SPECIAL 'N' QUICK ICED TEA

This is a tangy carbonated version of the classic iced tea.

6 tea bags
3 cups boiling water
1 bottle (28 ounces) 7-Up
Wafer-thin lemon, lime, or orange slices,
    for garnish

1. Place the tea bags in a teapot and add the boiling water. Stir, and allow to steep for 3 to 5 minutes.

2. Pour the tea into a large pitcher and chill. When ready to serve, stir in the 7-Up.

3. Serve over ice cubes in tall glasses, garnished with a fruit slice.

SERVINGS: 6 TALL GLASSES

LIME 'N' LEMONADE

A wonderful way to welcome summer guests of all ages to a garden banquet.

5 cups water
1½ cups sugar
½ cup fresh lemon juice
1 can (6 ounces) frozen limeade
    concentrate
2 bottles (12 ounces each) ginger ale
Mint sprigs, for garnish

1. Combine the water and sugar in a medium-size saucepan and place over moderate heat. Cook, stirring, until the sugar is dissolved. Set aside to cool.

2. Stir the lemon juice and limeade concentrate (undiluted) into the sugar syrup, mixing thoroughly. Pour into a large pitcher or a punch bowl.

3. Just before serving, add some ice and stir in the ginger ale. Add mint sprigs as garnish.

SERVINGS: 16 PUNCH CUPS

HAWAIIAN HULA SHAKE

Great for a summer luau, this shake has all those great paradise island flavors.

1 cup fresh coconut milk
    (see page 30, or canned
    unsweetened coconut milk)
1 cup pineapple juice
1 teaspoon coconut extract
½ cup chocolate syrup
1 cup vanilla ice cream
Maraschino cherries and pineapple
    chunks skewered on toothpicks,
    for garnish

1. Put all the ingredients, through the ice cream, in a blender and blend on medium speed until smooth, 15 seconds.

2. Pour into tall frosted glasses. Add a cherry-and-pineapple garnish to each.

SERVINGS: 4 TALL GLASSES

MOLLY PITCHER

Ever wonder how to glorify barbecued hot dogs? This is it! You can make this a July Fourth Special by serving it over ice cube flags. See the instructions for ice, page 2.

2 cups cranberry juice cocktail
2 cups pineapple juice
¼ teaspoon almond extract
1 quart 7-Up

1. Place the juices and the almond extract in a large pitcher. Mix well and refrigerate.

2. Just before serving, add the 7-Up, stir, and pour over ice in tall glasses.

SERVINGS: 8 TALL GLASSES

TROPICAL CUCUMBER

Perfect for taking to the beach in a cooler. This recipe makes a large quantity—it'll keep nicely in the refrigerator.

2 cups sugar
2 quarts cold water
Zest of 2 lemons
1½ cups fresh lemon juice (8 lemons)
1 cup fresh lime juice (6 limes)
1 cup thinly sliced cucumber
Lemonade ice cubes (see this page)
Fresh mint leaves, for garnish

1. Combine the sugar and 2 cups of the water in a medium-size saucepan. Boil for 1 minute. Remove from the heat.

2. Add the lemon zest to the sugar syrup and allow to steep for 7 minutes. Remove the zest.

3. Add the remaining 6 cups water, the lemon and lime juices, and the cucumber to the sugar syrup. Stir well and chill.

4. Just before leaving for the beach, put some lemonade ice cubes in a cooler jug and add the punch. Take along some mint leaves for garnish, if you like.

SERVINGS: 12 PLASTIC TUMBLERS

FLAVORED ICE CUBES

Punches and other iced drinks taste even better if the ice used to chill them is flavored. Freeze lemonade, cranberry juice, grape juice—or any of your favorites—in ice cube trays and add them to fruit punches and iced teas. Freeze coffee to add to iced coffee and chocolate sodas. No more watery drinks!

SUMMER DELIGHT

Orange and chocolate together is a delicious combination, but it's unusual to find them blended into a drink. Enjoy this by itself or serve light orange wafers alongside.

2 cups orange juice, preferably fresh
1 pint chocolate ice cream
1 quart ginger ale
Grate orange zest and maraschino
cherries, for garnish

1. Place the orange juice and ice cream in a blender. Blend on medium speed until smooth, 30 seconds.

2. Fill tall glasses three-quarters full with crushed ice. Fill each glass halfway with ginger ale, then add the blender mixture, stirring gently.

3. Garnish with grated orange zest and a maraschino cherry.

SERVINGS: 8 TALL GLASSES

CABANA DELIGHT

Scoop this out at the beach or at poolside for thirsty swimmers and sun worshipers.

2 cups orange juice, preferably fresh
2 cups cold milk
2 eggs (see Note, page 34)
½ cup honey
1 banana, cut in pieces
1 pint vanilla ice cream
Maraschino cherries, for garnish

1. Place all the ingredients through the banana in a blender and blend on medium speed until smooth, 1 minute.

2. Pour into tall glasses over cracked ice, add a scoop of ice cream, and top with a cherry.

SERVINGS: 6 TALL GLASSES

THE PINK SNOWMAN

This is so beautiful and delicious. Serve it in delicate goblets or tall soda glasses.

1 cup orange juice, preferably fresh
1 package (10 ounces) frozen strawberries,
  partially thawed
½ cup water
2 large scoops vanilla ice cream
Strawberries or orange slices,
  for garnish

1. Place the juice, berries, and water in a blender and blend on medium speed until smooth, 30 seconds.

2. Pour into tall glasses or goblets, and add a scoop of ice cream to each. Garnish with fruit, add a straw, and serve immediately.

SERVINGS: 2 LARGE GOBLETS

ORANGE SWIZZLE

Tart and tangy, nothing refreshes like this orange juice-ginger ale combo.

1 can (6½ ounces) frozen
  orange juice
  concentrate, thawed
1 quart ginger ale
Orange slices and maraschino cherries,
  for garnish

1. Fill 4 tall glasses with ice cubes.

2. Place a heaping tablespoon of orange juice concentrate in each glass, and fill with ginger ale. Stir to blend thoroughly.

3. Top with orange slices and cherries, add a decorative straw, and serve.

SERVINGS: 4 TALL GLASSES

BERRY GRANITÉ

Whenever it's berry-picking time in your home town—or at least when the berries hit the market in abundance—set some aside for this refreshing icy granité.

1 quart fresh strawberries,
*   rinsed and hulled, or*
*   1 quart fresh raspberries,*
*   rinsed*
3 cups sugar
1 tablespoon strawberry
*   (or raspberry) extract*
2 cups water
Sliced strawberries or whole raspberries,
*   for garnish*

1. Place the berries in a shallow bowl and cover with the sugar. Set aside to form a syrup, about 1 hour.

2. Once the syrup has formed, place a sieve over a medium-size bowl and pour the berries and syrup through, pressing with a wooden spoon to extract all the juice and syrup.

3. Add the extract and the water and mix well. Pour into a freezer container and freeze until a light frosting appears, about 2 hours.

4. Spoon into small glasses, garnished with strawberry slices or whole raspberries.

SERVINGS: 4 SMALL GLASSES

FRUIT GRANITÉS

Summer fruits make refreshing "granités," a favorite drink in France that was adopted from the Italian "graniti." The granité resembles snow-frosted water. It must always be liquid enough to be poured into a glass.

ORANGE GRANITÉ

12 oranges, approximately
2 cups sugar
1 quart water
Maraschino cherries, orange slices,
*   or lemon slices, for garnish*

1. Peel 6 oranges cleanly. Slice the peeled oranges, remove any seeds, and place the slices in a wide bowl. Sprinkle with the sugar. Set aside to make a syrup, 3 hours.

2. Once the syrup has formed, place a sieve over a medium-size bowl and pour the orange slices and syrup through, pressing with a wooden spoon to extract all the juice and syrup. Squeeze the juice from the other 6 oranges, or as many as it takes to yield about 3 cups, and add it to the syrup.

3. Add the water, mix well, and strain into a freezer container. Freeze until a light frosting appears, about 2 hours.

4. Spoon into small glasses, garnished with fruit.

SERVINGS: 8 TO 10 SMALL GLASSES

MY THREE SUNS

A bright refresher. Quick, elegant, and scrumptious!

2 cups orange juice, preferably
*   fresh*
1 quart apple juice
1 pint strawberry sherbet
Strips of orange zest, for garnish

1. Pour the orange juice and apple juice into a large pitcher and stir well.

2. Fill tall frosted glasses with cracked ice, and add the juice.

3. Top each glass with a scoop of sherbet, garnish with orange zest, and add a straw.

SERVINGS: 8 TALL GLASSES

MELONADE

A beautiful addition to any summer party, especially when served in a melon bowl.

> *1 medium-size ripe watermelon*
> *1 cup lemon juice, preferably fresh*
> *2 cups orange juice, preferably fresh*
> *2 cups sugar dissolved in*
> > *2 cups hot water, or 2 cups prepared*
> > *sugar syrup (see page 69)*
>
> *2 bottles (28 ounces each) 7-Up*
> *Dash of grenadine syrup (optional)*
> *Lime slices, whole small strawberries,*
> > *or a combination of sliced oranges*
> > *and bananas, for garnish*

1. Cut the watermelon in half, forming a zigzag-edge cut. Remove the pulp, discarding the seeds. Purée the pulp, in batches, in a blender. This should yield about 6 cups of juice. Set one melon half aside to be the punch bowl (see Watermelon Punch Bowl, this page).

2. Combine the watermelon juice, the lemon and orange juices, and the sugar syrup in a large pitcher. Stir well.

3. When ready to serve, place some ice cubes in the melon bowl and add the juice mixture. Carefully mix in the 7-Up. You may want to add some grenadine for color.

4. Garnish the punch with fruit, and ladle into punch cups.

SERVINGS: 30 PUNCH CUPS

WATERMELON PUNCH BOWL

A watermelon makes a decorative container for any kind of party punch—especially pretty if you use pink or green or clear glass punch cups.

Using a sharp knife, cut 1½-inch zigzags around the center of the melon from end to end. Be sure to cut as deep into the melon as you can. Pull the melon apart and scoop out the pulp with a large spoon.

You can use both parts if you cut the melon perfectly in half. Or for one large bowl, make the cut closer to the top so you have a deeper bowl.

NECTAR OF NECTARINES

Fresh and fruity, cool and fast. Try this also with peaches, blueberries, blackberries, strawberries, or raspberries. It can be stored in the refrigerator or taken along in a small thermos.

3 or 4 nectarines, peeled
*   and sliced, to make 1 cup slices*
½ cup fresh orange juice
1 tablespoon lemon juice, preferably fresh
1 tablespoon sugar
1 cup finely cracked ice

Place all the ingredients in a blender and blend on medium speed until smooth, about 1 minute.

SERVINGS: 1 TALL GLASS

FAST FRUIT PUNCH

This punch can be carried in a cooler to beaches, streams, fields, games, and gatherings of every kind. You may lose the fizz from the ginger ale, but not the flavor. If you are taking it in a cooler, make sure all the ingredients are well chilled first. You can make lemonade ice cubes (see page 61) instead of stirring in the lemonade—that way the flavor won't be diluted in the summer sun!

1 can (6 ounces) frozen orange juice
*   concentrate*
1 can (6 ounces) frozen lemonade
*   concentrate*
1 quart ginger ale
1 large can (46 ounces) pineapple juice
1 bottle (32 ounces) grape juice
Fresh fruit of any kind, for garnish

Prepare the orange juice and lemonade according to the directions on the can. Combine them, along with the ginger ale, pineapple juice, and grape juice, in a large punch bowl and stir gently. Add ice and the fruit garnish.

SERVINGS: 26 PAPER CUPS (6 OUNCE CUPS)

TALL PAUL

When you're starving and dinner is still a long way off, this is the drink to whip up.

2 cups orange juice,
preferably fresh,
chilled
1 banana, cut in pieces
1 cup heavy (whipping)
cream
Orange slices, for garnish

Place the juice, banana, and cream in a blender and blend for 15 seconds at high speed. Pour into tall glasses and top each with an orange slice.

SERVINGS: 2 TALL GLASSES

HANDYMAN'S PUNCH

A tea-based punch—good for a September beach crowd, when fresh apple cider is on hand.

2 cups extra-strong tea, chilled
1 quart apple cider
¼ cup fresh lemon juice
1 quart ginger ale, chilled
Wafer-thin lemon slices, for garnish

1. Combine the tea, cider, and lemon juice in a punch bowl and stir.

2. Just before serving, add some ice cubes and stir in the ginger ale. Top with lemon slices.

SERVINGS: 24 PUNCH
CUPS

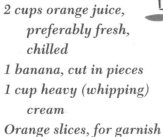

RHUBARB PUNCH

Rhubarb is an unexpected punch ingredient, but a lovely one. This is a bit time-consuming to make, but your efforts will be rewarded by lavish praise from your guests.

> *1½ pounds fresh rhubarb, trimmed*
> *   of leaves and cut into small pieces*
> *1 quart water*
> *1½ cups sugar*
> *½ cup orange juice, preferably fresh*
> *Juice of 1 lemon*
> *Pinch of salt*
> *1 quart ginger ale*
> *Fresh mint leaves, for garnish*

1. Combine the rhubarb and the water in a large saucepan, and bring to a boil. Cook, partially covered, over medium-high heat until the fruit is soft, 10 minutes. Strain into another saucepan. (You may reserve the pulp for another use.) Add the sugar to the strained juice and heat to boiling, stirring to mix well. Set aside to cool.

2. Add the orange juice, lemon juice, and salt. Refrigerate until ready to serve.

3. Just before serving, place some ice in a punch bowl, pour in the punch, and add the ginger ale. Top with mint leaves.

SERVINGS: 12 PUNCH CUPS

SUGAR SYRUP

Here's a ready-made sweetener for fresh fruit drinks.

3 cups water
3 cups sugar

Boil sugar and water together in a medium saucepan for 5 minutes. Store in a covered container in the refrigerator after cooling for up to 1 week.

CREOLE LEMONADE

An old Creole recipe, this makes a glorious summer punch.

2 pineapples
2 cups sugar
3 quarts water
Juice of 12 lemons
2 quarts seltzer or club soda
12 lemons, sliced very thin
1 pint fresh ripe strawberries, rinsed
    and hulled

1. Quarter, peel, core, and coarsely chop one of the pineapples. Place it in a blender and blend to purée. Halve, peel, and core the other pineapple, and cut it into 36 thin slices.

2. Combine the sugar, water, lemon juice, and pineapple juice in a large punch bowl. Mix well.

3. When you are ready to serve, place a large block of ice in the punch bowl and stir in the seltzer. Add the lemon slices, pineapple slices, and strawberries.

4. Place some crushed ice in each punch cup, and then fill with lemonade.

SERVINGS: 30 PUNCH CUPS

WAGON WHEELS

Orange slices make great garnishes, cheering up even the simplest of fruit drinks, including a mix of equal amounts of orange juice and apple cider. Scrub the peel of a whole orange well under cool running water, then pat dry with paper towels. Cut the orange into neat 1/4-inch slices, so that they look like wagon wheels. Center a maraschino cherry on each side of an orange slice and anchor them with a toothpick. Repeat with the remaining slices.

JIMMY'S CLASSIC LIMEADE

Frost some tall, thin glasses for this standby thirst quencher.

¼ cup fresh lime juice
2 tablespoons sugar, or ¼ cup
*   sugar syrup (see page 69)*
1 cup cold water
Mint sprig, for garnish

Combine the lime juice, sugar or sugar syrup, and water in a small bowl or pitcher. Stir well, and serve over ice cubes in a tall glass. Top with a sprig of mint.

SERVINGS: 1 TALL GLASS

THE SOUTHERN BELLE

Don't even bother to try this one if you are not a chocolate-lover. P.S.: Allow yourself to feel guilty for ten minutes only!

2 generous tablespoons chocolate
*   ice cream*
2 tablespoons fudge topping
1 cup milk
6 Thin Mints or other chocolate-covered
*   mint after-dinner patties*
Maraschino cherries or chocolate
*   shavings, for garnish*

1. Put the ice cream, fudge topping, and milk in a blender. Blend for 30 seconds.

2. Break the chocolate mint patties into pieces, add to the blender, and blend for 10 seconds.

3. Pour into goblets, and garnish each with a cherry or chocolate shavings.

SERVINGS: 1 TALL GLASS

EASY MEXICAN COFFEE

This is good for any kind of crowd, any time of the year—but it especially livens up a Fourth of July celebration.

1 vanilla bean
3 long cinnamon sticks (5 inches each)
¾ cup espresso or dark-roasted coffee
*   grounds*
10 cups cold water
½ cup heavy (whipping) cream
Dark brown sugar, to taste

1. Place the vanilla bean and cinnamon sticks in the bottom of a coffeepot, and brew the coffee by any method, using the 10 cups of water. Discard the grounds. Keep the coffee hot.

2. Whip the cream, adding brown sugar to taste, until stiff.

3. Pour the hot coffee into cups, and top each with some whipped cream.

SERVINGS: 16 COFFEE CUPS

CHERRY JUBILEE

You might try this one as a liquid dessert following a summer dinner. If you're being mindful of calories, blend in a low- or nonfat ice cream. The drink will be just as luscious.

2 cups strong coffee, chilled
½ pint cherry ice cream
1 tablespoon maraschino
cherry juice
Maraschino cherries, for garnish

1. Place the coffee, ice cream, and cherry juice in a blender and blend on medium speed until smooth, 30 seconds.

2. Pour into chilled punch cups and top each with a cherry.

SERVINGS: 4 PUNCH CUPS

AUDREY'S SPICED AND ICED COFFEE

Audrey's recipes are the best! Try this winsome blend of spices and coffee.

1 cinnamon stick (3 inches)
4 whole cloves
6 tablespoons sugar
4 cups strong hot coffee
Vanilla ice cream or heavy (whipping)
    cream, for garnish

1. Add the spices and sugar to the hot coffee. Stir, and let it cool to room temperature. Then pour into a glass pitcher and chill in the refrigerator.

2. Remove the cloves and cinnamon stick, and serve over ice in tall glasses, with a bit of ice cream or heavy cream stirred in.

SERVINGS: 4 TALL GLASSES

LEMON COFFEE

This recipe is for two tall servings and is perfect late in the afternoon. By increasing the quantities, you will have a very good punch for any occasion.

2 cups strong coffee,
    chilled
1 cup lemon sherbet, slightly softened
1 tablespoon grated
    lemon zest
1 tablespoon lemon juice,
    preferably fresh
2 tablespoons sugar
Maraschino cherries, for garnish

Place all the ingredients, through the sugar, in a blender and blend on medium speed for 2 minutes. Serve in frosted glasses, garnished with a cherry.

SERVINGS: 2 TALL GLASSES

RUTH'S RICO CHICO

A savory Mexican coffee—just perfect for topping off an intimate outdoor dinner.

> 2 tablespoons chocolate syrup
> ½ cup heavy (whipping) cream
> ¼ teaspoon ground cinnamon
> 2 tablespoons sugar
> Pinch of grated nutmeg
> 2 cups strong hot coffee
> Whipped cream and
>   ground cinnamon,
>   for garnish

1. Place the chocolate syrup, cream, cinnamon, sugar, and nutmeg in a blender. Pulse twice, then blend to thicken, about 1 minute.

2. Pour the hot coffee into 4 mugs and add the syrup mixture to each, stirring gently. Top with whipped cream, and sprinkle with extra cinnamon.

SERVINGS: 4 MUGS

ASIAN ICED COFFEE

Cardamom gives this drink its unusual flavor. Serve it with some exotic pastries.

> 4 cups cold water
> 1 teaspoon cardamom seeds
> ½ cup drip-grind coffee
> Sugar, to taste
> Pineapple cubes, for garnish

1. Place the water and cardamom seeds in a medium-size saucepan and bring to a boil over high heat. Continue boiling, uncovered, for 3 minutes.

2. Meanwhile, set up a drip coffeepot with the measured amount of ground coffee.

3. Pour the cardamom water over the coffee grounds. Sweeten the coffee to taste and allow it to cool.

4. Strain over ice in tall glasses, and garnish each one with a pineapple cube.

SERVINGS: 4 TALL GLASSES

CAMPFIRE COFFEE

For hunting and fishing trips, wilderness adventures, and any other adventures around the campfire.

5 quarts plus 1 cup cold water
1½ cups regular-grind coffee
1 egg

1. In a large pot set over a charcoal fire or campfire, bring the 5 quarts of water to a rolling boil.

2. Place the coffee, egg, and ½ cup of cold water in a bowl and mix well. Pour this mixture into the boiling water and let it return to a boil.

3. Immediately remove the pot from the heat and add the last ½ cup of cold water. The coffee grounds will sink to the bottom of the pot.

4. Ladle the coffee into tin mugs or paper cups.

SERVINGS: 30 SMALL MUGS

MIDGE'S MUDSLIDE SMOOTHIE

This cooling drink is big on flavor, and it's a good substitute for dessert if you're entertaining the caffeine-conscious or calorie-counters. You can prepare and refrigerate it several hours in advance.

2 cups crushed ice
2 cups double-strength decaffeinated
    coffee, chilled
1 teaspoon vanilla extract
1 cup vanilla low-fat yogurt
Ground cinnamon, to taste (optional)

1. Combine the crushed ice, coffee, and vanilla extract in a blender and blend until smooth.

2. Add the yogurt and blend for 10 seconds.

3. Pour into parfait glasses or goblets, and sprinkle lightly with cinnamon, if desired.

SERVINGS: 4 PARFAIT GLASSES

SCHOOL DAYS, SCHOOL DAYS

Good old golden rule days. This is the time of year when you move indoors and extend an autumn welcome to your friends. If you've tended a garden, chances are you have a bushel or two of tomatoes just waiting to be cooked up in an exciting spicy drink. And with the harvest just beginning in the apple orchards and cranberry bogs, fresh cider and cranberries are everywhere, and fall is in the air.

School box lunches need a thermos with a treat. Halloween is on the horizon—tiny thirsty trick-or-treaters appear on your threshold. Thanksgiving festivities spark your flair for entertaining—try Cucumber Punch as an appetizer, or a giant bowl of Pilgrim's Cider, or the Family Thanksgiving Punch, the ultimate in color and flavor.

HOMEMADE SPICY TOMATO JUICE

This is a great way to use up the not-so-perfect tomatoes in your own garden or to take advantage of by-the-bushel bargains at a farm market. You'll have enough juice to get you through all the bleak days of winter. (If you don't have the equipment for canning, reduce the quantities and make just enough for a great Thanksgiving dinner appetizer—and maybe extra for a day or two after.)

½ *bushel ripe tomatoes, rinsed*
and quartered
6 *large carrots, cut in pieces*
2 *large green bell peppers,*
stemmed,
seeded, and cut in pieces
4 *medium onions, chopped*
½ *bunch celery, cleaned and*
cut in pieces
1 *bunch parsley, rinsed*
Worcestershire sauce, to taste
Garlic powder, to taste
Salt and freshly ground black pepper,
to taste
Lemon juice, sugar, or onion juice
(optional)

1. Place the vegetables and the parsley in a large soup pot and bring to a boil (the tomato liquid will boil). Reduce the heat and simmer until soft, 30 minutes.

2. Place a colander in a large bowl and pour the vegetables and juice through it, pressing down hard to extract all the liquid.

3. Flavor the juice to taste with Worcestershire sauce, garlic powder, and salt and pepper, and add lemon juice, sugar, or onion juice, if desired. Can in airtight jars following your usual canning instructions.

4. Serve over crushed ice, with an additional seasoning of lemon or onion juice, or some sugar.

SERVINGS: 12 QUARTS (48 SMALL GLASSES)

CUPBOARD KEEPER:
TOMATO JUICE À LA BLENDER

Blend any of the following combinations into a cup of tomato or tomato-vegetable juice for a low-calorie taste treat.

◆ *¼ cup chopped cucumber*
  Salt and freshly ground black pepper, to taste

◆ *½ cup chopped green bell pepper*
  Dash of onion juice
  Dash of Tabasco sauce
  Salt and freshly ground black pepper, to taste

◆ *2 fresh basil leaves, or ½ teaspoon dried basil*
  1 teaspoon chopped onion
  Dash of Tabasco sauce
  Salt and freshly ground black pepper, to taste

◆ *1 clove garlic, chopped*
  Dash of fresh lemon juice
  Salt and freshly ground black pepper, to taste

◆ *3 tablespoons lime juice, preferably fresh*
  Dash of Tabasco sauce

◆ *½ cup clam juice*
  1 tablespoon lime juice, preferably fresh
  Dash of Worcestershire sauce

◆ *½ cup plain yogurt*
  1 tablespoon chopped onion
  Salt and freshly ground black pepper, to taste

SUNSET SAUCE

A hearty tomato drink with a healthy spark of tart citrus.

> *10 ounces stewed tomatoes,*
> *   homemade or canned*
> *2 tablespoons lemon juice,*
> *   preferably fresh*
> *2 tablespoons lime juice, preferably fresh*
> *1 cup cold water*
> *Wafer-thin lime slices, for garnish*

1. Place the stewed tomatoes and the juices in a blender and blend for 30 seconds on medium speed.

2. Add the cold water, stir, and pour into old-fashioned glasses filled with crushed ice. Garnish each with a slice of lime.

SERVINGS: 6 OLD-FASHIONED GLASSES

THE BUFFALO CHILL

Wildly spicy and delectable. Serve this at a fall picnic (bring it along in a thermos) or at a backyard gathering.

1 large can (46 ounces) tomato juice
1 cucumber, peeled and grated
3 scallions, trimmed and finely chopped
¼ cup lemon juice, preferably fresh
2 tablespoons Worcestershire sauce
Dash of Tabasco sauce
Pinch of garlic salt
Salt and freshly ground
*   black pepper,*
*   to taste*
Parsley sprigs, for garnish

1. Place all the ingredients, through the salt and pepper, in a large pitcher and stir. Refrigerate for 1 hour.

2. Before serving, strain the juice into another pitcher. Then pour it into old-fashioned glasses, and garnish each with a parsley sprig.

SERVINGS: 8 OLD-FASHIONED GLASSES

TOMATO HURRY-CURRY

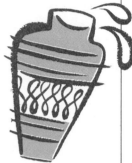

Pack this up to take to the beach along with a bag of peanuts for an energizing end-of-the-season treat.

1 large can (46 ounces)
*   tomato juice*
1 teaspoon curry powder
Dash of Tabasco sauce

1. Place ½ cup of the tomato juice in a small bowl, add the curry powder, and stir well to blend. Put this mixture into a large saucepan and add the remaining tomato juice and the Tabasco. Heat just to boiling. Refrigerate.

2. Pour the chilled juice into a thermos just before you leave for the beach.

SERVINGS: 6 TO 8 PAPER CUPS OR MUGS

CUCUMBER PUNCH

Cucumbers are abundant at the end of the summer and can be prepared a number of ways for tasty drinks. This one is a good, hearty punch, perfect for a fall luncheon.

> *1 can (10½ ounces) condensed*
> *tomato soup*
> *2 cups buttermilk*
> *½ teaspoon curry powder*
> *½ teaspoon Worcestershire sauce*
> *3 cucumbers, peeled and finely diced*
> *Cucumber slices and freshly ground black*
> *pepper, for garnish*

1. Place the soup, buttermilk, and seasonings in a blender and blend for 30 seconds on low speed. Add the diced cucumber and stir.

2. Pour into glass mugs, and top with cucumber slices and a sprinkling of black pepper.

SERVINGS: 6 MUGS

CELERY, ANYONE?

For a tasty, nourishing vegetable highball, combine celery and tomato juices.

> *2 cups tomato or tomato-vegetable juice*
> *1 cup celery juice*
> *Stuffed green olives, for garnish*

Combine the juices in a pitcher and stir well. Serve in tall glasses, with an olive or two in each.

SERVINGS: 2 TALL GLASSES

BABY ROY'S CHOCOLATE PEPPERMINT

A great birthday party drink. Children love this one, especially when it's served with a peppermint candy stirrer.

> *1 can (4½ ounces) chocolate syrup*
> *1 quart cold milk*
> *1 teaspoon peppermint extract*
> *1 pint chocolate ice cream,*
>   *softened*
> *Whipped cream and peppermint*
>   *sticks, for garnish*

Place all the ingredients, through the ice cream, in a blender and blend until smooth, 1 minute. Pour into tall glasses, top with whipped cream, and add a candy stirrer to each.

SERVINGS: 6 TALL GLASSES

CUPBOARD KEEPERS: CHOCOLATE PLUS

For a great flavor, add any one of the following to a cup of cold chocolate milk or hot cocoa:

◆ **Wedge of lemon, lime, or orange (squeezed into cocoa made with water only)**

◆ **Dash of vanilla, almond, or rum extract**

◆ **1 teaspoon cherry, raspberry, or strawberry syrup**

◆ **1 heaping tablespoon vanilla ice cream**

◆ **Use a candy cane for a stirrer**

◆ **Float mini-marshmallows**

◆ **Top with grated chocolate or coconut**

CHOCOLATE MALTED MILK SHAKE

The kind of thick, rich, really special smoothie that your grandfather remembers.

¼ cup malt powder (see Note)
½ cup chocolate syrup
2 large scoops chocolate ice cream
1½ cups cold milk

Combine all the ingredients in a blender or milk-shake machine. Blend on medium speed for 2 minutes, and pour into tall glasses.

SERVINGS: 2 TALL GLASSES

Note: Malt powder isn't as easy to find as it once was, but it is carried in major supermarkets, next to the cocoa powder and hot chocolate mixes.

DYNAMITE CHOCOLATE DRAGONS

At teenage parties or sleepovers during the holidays, make any number of these.

⅓ cup chocolate syrup
1½ cups cold milk
2 teaspoons sugar
1 cup vanilla ice cream
Grated chocolate, for garnish

Place the syrup, milk, sugar, and ice cream in a blender and blend until smooth. Pour into tall glasses, and top with the grated chocolate.

SERVINGS: 2 TALL GLASSES

PEANUT BUTTER 'N' JELLY

This is a drinkable sandwich. Children love it!

4 cups cold milk
1 cup peanut butter
1 teaspoon vanilla extract
2 tablespoons currant jelly
1 pint chocolate ice cream

1. Place half of each of the ingredients in a blender and blend until smooth. Pour the mixture into a pitcher, and repeat with the other half.

2. Serve in tall glasses, each with a different colored straw.

SERVINGS: 6 TALL GLASSES

CRANBERRY CREAM SHAKE

A milk shake with a cranberry-orange flavor. Beware, this could be habit-forming—especially for those with a taste for the tart!

1 small can (4 ounces) whole-berry cranberry sauce
1 quart orange juice
1 pint vanilla ice cream, softened
Orange slices, for garnish

1. Combine half of the cranberry sauce, juice, and ice cream in a blender. Blend on medium speed until smooth, 30 seconds. Pour into a pitcher, and repeat with the other half.

2. Pour into tall glasses, and perch a slice of orange on the rim of each one.

SERVINGS: 6 TALL GLASSES

BANANA COFFEE SMOOTHIE

For the adult crowd. Give this a whirl in your blender, and chances are you will make it again and again. It, too, works well with nonfat frozen yogurt.

2 or 3 bananas, cut in pieces
2 cups coffee, chilled
1 pint vanilla ice cream, softened
1 teaspoon vanilla extract
⅓ cup sugar
Maraschino cherries, for garnish

Put all the ingredients, through the sugar, in a blender. Blend at medium speed for 1 minute. Serve in frosted mugs or glasses, topped with a cherry.

SERVINGS: 4 MUGS

BANANA MILK SMOOTHIE

Make this luscious smoothie with low-fat milk and nonfat frozen yogurt, or go all out and blend up the full-calorie version. Either way, it goes down the hatch really easily.

2 cups milk
2 bananas, cut in pieces
1 pint vanilla ice cream, softened
Grated nutmeg, for garnish

Put the milk, bananas, and ice cream in a blender. Blend on high speed until smooth, 1 minute. Pour into tall glasses, and sprinkle with nutmeg.

SERVINGS: 6 TALL GLASSES

BARRISTER'S DESSERT SHAKE

This delicate combination of coffee and banana—sweet and creamy—is actually dessert and after-dinner coffee all in one!

> *½ cup light cream or half-and-half*
> *2 cups strong coffee, chilled*
> *4 teaspoons sugar*
> *2 bananas, sliced*
> *Shredded coconut, for garnish*

Combine all the ingredients, through the bananas, in a blender and blend on high speed until smooth. Serve topped with a bit of shredded coconut.

SERVINGS: 4 GLASSES

MONKEY SEE, MONKEY DO

Buy a can of cream of coconut at the grocery store and try this out on the kids when they're taking a homework break. You will soon be making seconds.

> *⅓ cup canned cream of coconut,*
> *   such as Coco Lopez*
> *½ cup lemon sherbet, softened*
> *2 cups 7-Up, chilled*
> *Wafer-thin lime*
> *   slices, for garnish*

1. Divide the cream of coconut and lemon sherbet between 2 tall glasses, and stir well.

2. Add a few ice cubes, and fill the glasses with 7-Up. Stir gently, and top each with a slice of lime.

SERVINGS: 2 TALL GLASSES

CRANBERRY SODA

This is a colorful and unusual drink—great to serve up when cranberry season starts.

2 cups fresh cranberries, rinsed
  and stemmed
1 cup water
Pinch of salt
1 cup sugar
1 pint vanilla ice cream
1 quart club soda

1. Place the cranberries, water, salt, and sugar in a medium-size saucepan. Bring to a boil. Reduce the heat and simmer until the cranberries burst and are soft, about 5 minutes. Set aside to cool.

2. When ready to serve, place a spoonful of ice cream in each tall glass. Add 2 or 3 teaspoons of the cranberry mixture, and fill the glass with club soda. Add a colored straw and stir gently.

SERVINGS: 6 TALL GLASSES

GINGER ALE FLOAT

Floats and sodas are thirst-quenching, and they can be made in a hurry. Don't forget to pass around the pretzels and peanuts with this cardplayer's delight.

2 cups orange juice, preferably fresh,
  chilled
2 cans (12 ounces each) ginger ale
1 pint chocolate ice cream
Grated orange zest, for garnish

Divide the orange juice and ginger ale among 6 tall frosted glasses. Stir to combine, then top each with a spoonful of ice cream and a sprinkling of orange zest.

SERVINGS: 6 TALL GLASSES

ORANGE ICE CREAM SODA

Brightly colored and delicious. Serve this as an after-school treat or as a dessert.

1 large can (12 ounces) frozen orange juice concentrate, thawed
½ cup light cream or half-and-half
1 quart ginger ale
1 pint vanilla ice cream
1 pint orange sherbet

1. Put a heaping teaspoon of orange juice concentrate in each glass.

2. Add 1 tablespoon light cream to each glass, and mix well.

3. Stir in ¼ cup ginger ale, and add 1 scoop each of the ice cream and the sherbet.

4. Fill the glasses with the remaining ginger ale. Stir gently, and serve with a straw and a long-handled spoon.

SERVINGS: 6 SODA GLASSES

GRAPE SHAKE

This is a very sweet milk shake, and because of its pretty lavender color it looks divine. Even if you make it for yourself, make it special by frosting your glass.

1 cup milk
½ cup grape juice
1 large scoop vanilla ice cream

Combine the milk, grape juice, and ice cream in a blender and blend for 1 minute on medium speed. Pour into a frosted glass or mug.

SERVINGS: 1 TALL GLASS

CHOCOLATE EGG CREAM

A New York favorite. You can still create an authentic egg cream drink by using whipped egg whites as they did in the "good old days." The egg whites were blended with chocolate syrup in the bottom of a very tall glass and then seltzer water was added to the mixture. Here is an easier way.

> 1 to 3 tablespoons chocolate syrup
> ½ cup cold milk or heavy (whipping)
>   cream
> Seltzer or club soda, chilled

Put the chocolate syrup in the bottom of a tall glass. Add the milk or heavy cream, and stir with a spoon. Fill the glass with seltzer or club soda, and stir well. Add a straw and slurp away.

SERVINGS: 1 TALL GLASS

Note: New Yorkers will tell you the traditional syrup for an egg cream is Fox's U-Bet. Look for it in large supermarkets.

OLD-FASHIONED ROOT BEER FLOAT

There's no trick to it . . .

Fill a glass three-quarters full with cold root beer. Top with a scoop of vanilla ice cream, and add a long-handled spoon and a straw. (To make it really deluxe, add a bit of whipped cream.)

For something a bit different, try a float using sarsaparilla or chocolate soda.

CHOCOLATE SPECTACULAR

A creamy-rich soda for all seasons.

3 cups cold milk
1 cup heavy (whipping) cream
1½ cups chocolate syrup
2 tablespoons sugar
1 teaspoon vanilla extract
1 quart club soda
Whipped cream and
*   maraschino cherries,*
*   for garnish*

1. Combine the milk, cream, chocolate syrup, sugar, and vanilla in a blender. Blend on medium speed for 30 seconds.

2. Place a few ice cubes in each of 4 glasses, and divide the blender mixture among them. Top each with club soda and stir gently. Add a dollop of whipped cream, top with a maraschino cherry, and insert a straw and a long-handled spoon.

SERVINGS: 6 TALL GLASSES

THE JESSE JAMES

Those he-man poker players will go wild for this one. Add club soda for fizz, if desired.

2 tablespoons powdered instant coffee
Pinch of salt
¼ cup sugar
1 quart milk
¼ teaspoon peppermint extract
2 pints vanilla ice cream
Chocolate shavings or maraschino
*   cherries, for garnish*

1. Combine the instant coffee, salt, and sugar in a large pitcher.

2. Add 1 cup of the milk and stir until the coffee and sugar are dissolved.

3. Add the remaining milk and the peppermint flavoring, and stir well.

4. Pour into soda glasses, top each with a scoop of ice cream, and add some chocolate shavings or a cherry. Insert a straw and a long-handled spoon.

SERVINGS: 4 SODA GLASSES

CRANBERRY JUICE

While it is certainly easy to have quart bottles on hand in your pantry, you can make your own fresh cranberry juice when the berries are available in the supermarket and store it in the freezer.

1 pound fresh cranberries, rinsed and
*   stemmed*
2 cups sugar
6 cups water

1. Place the cranberries, sugar, and water in a medium-size saucepan and bring to a boil. Reduce the heat and simmer until the cranberries burst and are soft, about 5 minutes.

2. Place a sieve over a bowl and line it with cheesecloth. Strain the cranberries through the cheesecloth, pressing to extract all the juice.

3. Cool and serve over ice, or refrigerate and use as needed.

SERVINGS: 4 TALL GLASSES

CRANBERRY JUBILEE PUNCH

Try out a quart of that homemade cranberry juice made special on some thirsty teenagers after the big game.

1 quart homemade cranberry juice or
*   store-bought cranberry juice*
*   cocktail, chilled*
1 quart lime sherbet
Wafer-thin lime slices, for garnish

Fill punch cups or paper cups with the cranberry juice. Add a heaping spoonful of sherbet, and top with a slice of lime.

SERVINGS:
12 SMALL
CUPS

CURRANT WATER

This is also delicious with raspberries and strawberries. Just follow the measurements and directions below.

> *½ pint ripe fresh currants*
> *1 quart water*
> *1 cup sugar*
> *Fresh currants, for garnish*

1. Stem the currants. Then place them in a medium-size bowl and crush them slightly by pressing with the back of a wooden spoon. Add just enough water to cover, and let stand for about 1 hour.

2. Strain the currants, reserving the liquid. Wrap the strained currants in a clean dish towel and squeeze it over the bowl of strained liquid. This should give you about 1 cup juice.

3. Add the quart of water and the sugar. Stir well and strain again, if necessary, this time into a pitcher that can be put on ice until you are ready to serve.

4. Garnish with extra whole currants.

SERVINGS: 6 SMALL GLASSES

BLACKBERRY DANDY

Taboo, Pictionary, Monopoly, and late-night card games will all be a little more exciting with this treat!

> *1 cup lemonade (made from concentrate)*
> *2 cups canned or frozen blackberries,*
> *   with juice*
> *1 cup club soda*
> *½ cup sugar*
> *1 quart ginger ale*
> *Strips of lemon zest, for garnish*

1. Place the lemonade, berries and juice, club soda, and sugar in a blender, and blend until smooth, 20 seconds.

2. Put some ice cubes in frosted tankards, and add the blender mixture until they are half filled.

3. Fill the tankards with ginger ale, stir, and serve topped with a lemon twist.

SERVINGS: 8 TANKARDS

ORANGE GROG

There's nothing like a thermos of grog at a chilly Saturday football game.

2 quarts fresh orange juice
1 cup sugar
3 cinnamon sticks (3 inches each)
20 whole cloves
3 tablespoons grated orange zest

1. Place all the ingredients in a large saucepan and bring to a boil. Reduce the heat and simmer for 5 minutes.

2. Strain the grog through a colander or sieve into a large pitcher, and then pour it into your thermos.

SERVINGS: 10 TO 12 MUGS

APPLE TREE TEA

Take this along for a tailgate picnic—the wonderful aroma alone will warm you up.

1 quart apple juice or cider
1 quart strong hot tea
Pinch of ground allspice
Pinch of ground cloves
Pinch of grated nutmeg
3 oranges, thinly sliced
3 lemons, thinly sliced
2 cinnamon sticks (3 inches each)
⅓ cup (packed) dark brown sugar
Strips of orange and lemon zest,
*   for garnish*

1. Place all the ingredients, through the brown sugar, in a large saucepan and bring to a boil. Reduce the heat and simmer for 10 minutes.

2. Strain into a thermos or preheated cups. Garnish with orange and lemon zest, if desired.

SERVINGS: 12 CUPS

PILGRIM'S CIDER

Throughout the fall season, this is a delicious and dependable punch to prepare. To save time, make it ahead, then warm it up just before serving. Guests will love it!

2 cups water
½ cup (packed) dark brown sugar
1 teaspoon grated orange zest
1 teaspoon coriander seeds
1 teaspoon ground allspice
¼ teaspoon grated nutmeg
2 teaspoons whole cloves
4 cinnamon sticks (3 inches each)
⅓ cup fresh lemon juice
2 quarts apple cider, warmed
Cinnamon sticks, for garnish

1. Place the water, brown sugar, orange zest, and spices in a small saucepan. Bring to a boil, reduce the heat, and simmer, covered, for 15 minutes.

2. Place a sieve or colander lined with cheesecloth over a large prewarmed punch bowl. Strain the spice mixture through the cheesecloth. Add the lemon juice and apple cider to the punch bowl, and stir.

3. Serve in punch cups, garnished with a cinnamon stick.

SERVINGS: 20 PUNCH CUPS

SPICE BAG

When you are preparing a warm punch that uses whole spices, make a little bag for the spices—it saves on messy straining. All you need is a little square of cheesecloth, about 5 x 5 inches, and a bit of string. Place the spices in the center of the square, bring all four corners together, and tie. When you are through brewing the hot drink, simply remove the bag and throw it away.

BETTY'S MULLED CIDER

My friend Betty serves this rich, aromatic punch at her terrific parties. We're all happy for the invitation!

5 cups cider
24 whole cloves
4 small cinnamon sticks (2 inches each)
4 cups grape juice
½ cup lemon juice, preferably fresh
2 quarts ginger ale (not chilled)
3 oranges, thinly sliced

1. Place the cider in a large saucepan and add the cloves and cinnamon sticks. Bring to a boil and simmer for 5 minutes.

2. Add the grape and lemon juices, stir, and pour into a punch bowl.

3. Pour in the ginger ale and stir gently. Add the orange slices.

SERVINGS: 24 PUNCH CUPS

DAPPER APPLE

When apples are plentiful in the fall, enjoy this unusual drink for a change of pace.

2 large apples, peeled, cored,
*   and cut into small pieces*
2 cups cold buttermilk
¼ cup sugar
¼ teaspoon ground cinnamon
Grated nutmeg or ground cinnamon,
*   for garnish*

Place the apple pieces, buttermilk, and sugar in a blender and blend until smooth, 1 minute. Pour into glasses, and sprinkle with nutmeg or cinnamon.

SERVINGS:
2 SMALL
GLASSES

THE CHILDREN'S HOUR

This is a really sweet, exceedingly delicious punch appreciated mostly by children. It's perfect for a birthday party or in a separate punch bowl for young guests at a gathering of family and friends.

2 quarts Hawaiian Punch, chilled
2 quarts cranberry juice cocktail, chilled
2 quarts cherry soda, chilled
1 pint strawberry sherbet, softened

Combine the Hawaiian Punch, cranberry juice, and cherry soda in a punch bowl. Add the sherbet and stir slowly to distribute it throughout.

SERVINGS: 40 PUNCH CUPS

PEACH PUNCH

Warm and tangy for Indian Summer.

1 large can (46 ounces) peach nectar
2 cups fresh orange juice
⅓ cup (packed) dark brown sugar
3 small cinnamon sticks (2 inches each), crumbled
6 whole cloves
2 tablespoons lime juice, preferably fresh
Grated orange zest, for garnish

1. Place the peach nectar, orange juice, and brown sugar in a large saucepan and bring to a boil. Reduce the heat to a simmer. Add the spices and stir until the sugar is dissolved, 5 minutes. Add the lime juice and stir.

2. Place a strainer over a prewarmed punch bowl and strain the punch into it.

3. Ladle into punch cups, and sprinkle each serving with a bit of orange zest.

SERVINGS: 12 PUNCH CUPS

WITCHIE STEW

A spooky brew—great for trick-or-treaters. (To really make it dramatic, just behind the punch bowl set a small container of dry ice with a bit of water added: it'll hiss and steam!)

1 cup orange juice, preferably fresh
6 whole cloves
3 cinnamon sticks (3 inches each)
3 quarts apple cider, chilled
2 pints orange sherbet
Miniature marshmallows, for garnish

1. Place the orange juice, cloves, and cinnamon sticks in a small saucepan and heat to boiling. Remove from the heat and set aside to cool.

2. Fill a large punch bowl with the cider. Add the seasoned orange juice and the sherbet. Stir gently.

3. Ladle into mini-mugs or paper cups, and top with mini-marshmallows.

SERVINGS: 24 SMALL MUGS

FISHMONGER'S PUNCH

Fast and easy—serve a batch and chill a batch. Great for a late September boiled lobster fest.

1 quart ginger ale
1 quart pineapple juice
1 bottle (16 ounces) grape juice
1 quart orange juice
1 quart lemonade (made from concentrate)

Combine all the ingredients in a punch bowl and mix well. Add a large block of ice or several trays of ice cubes.

SERVINGS: 28 PUNCH CUPS

HAWAIIAN COFFEE PUNCH

Here's another way to use Hawaiian Punch, in a real taste pleaser—for grown-ups this time!

2 cups strong coffee, chilled
2 cups Hawaiian Punch
1 pint vanilla ice cream
1 quart strawberry soda
Pineapple cubes, for garnish

1. Place half of the coffee, Hawaiian Punch, and ice cream in a blender. Blend on high speed for 30 seconds.

2. Place the remaining coffee, Hawaiian Punch, and ice cream in a punch bowl. Add the blender mixture and the strawberry soda. Stir gently.

3. Place a pineapple cube in each punch cup, and fill with the punch.

SERVINGS: 16 PUNCH CUPS

SPARKLING CITRUS PUNCH

Put a winner on the table at the next fraternity or sorority fund-raiser.

2 cans (6 ounces each) frozen limeade
*   concentrate, thawed*
1 quart unsweetened grapefruit juice
1 teaspoon bitters (see Note, page 36)
1 quart club soda, chilled
Wafer-thin lime slices, for garnish

1. Combine the limeade concentrate (undiluted), juice, and bitters in a large punch bowl and mix well.

2. Just before serving, add some ice cubes and the club soda. Mix thoroughly.

3. Serve in salt-rimmed frosted cups (see page 50), garnished with lime slices.

SERVINGS: 16 PUNCH CUPS

FAMILY THANKSGIVING PUNCH

The ultimate in color and cranberry flavor, this aromatic punch is accented with other fruit juices and delicately spiced.

1 quart water
¼ teaspoon grated nutmeg
1 teaspoon whole cloves
1 teaspoon coriander seeds
6 cinnamon sticks (3 inches each)
2 quarts cranberry juice cocktail
2 cups pineapple juice
4 cups grapefruit juice
1 cup raisins, for garnish

1. Combine the water and spices in a large saucepan, bring to a boil, and simmer for 15 minutes.

2. Add the juices and bring just to boiling. Remove from the heat.

3. Strain the punch through a sieve or colander into a large preheated punch bowl. Place a few raisins in each cup before serving the punch.

SERVINGS: 28 TO 30 PUNCH CUPS

HOT STUFF

Heating your mugs or punch bowl before adding a hot drink helps keep the drink hot and tasty.

◆ *Rinse them out under hot tap water and dry quickly and thoroughly, then fill.*

◆ *For a large group, put them in the dishwasher on the "dry" cycle, and leave them there until you need them.*

◆ *Put them on an electric hot tray until you are ready to serve.*

MERRY BERRY

A warm and inviting punch for a harvest table, a teachers' tea, or a Thanksgiving Day feast.

1 quart cranberry-apple drink
2 cups water
1 cup sugar
6 cinnamon sticks (3 inches each)
10 whole cloves
Zest of 1 lemon, cut in thin strips
¼ cup fresh lemon juice
Apples slices, for garnish

1. Combine the cranberry-apple drink, water, sugar, spices, and lemon zest in a large saucepan. Bring to a boil, reduce the heat, and simmer for 10 minutes.

2. Place a sieve or colander over a large bowl or pitcher. Strain the cranberry punch through this, and set it aside to cool for 15 minutes.

3. Add the lemon juice and stir. Pour the punch into a punch bowl.

4. Place apple slices in each punch cup before serving the punch.

SERVINGS: 16 PUNCH CUPS

CROCKPOT CRANBERRY

Have this ready to warm the crew when they return from ice skating.

2 cups cranberry juice cocktail
2 quarts apple cider
½ cup sugar
1 orange studded with 6 whole cloves
2 cinnamon sticks (3 inches each)
Orange slices or cinnamon sticks,
   for garnish

Combine all the ingredients in a crockpot, and simmer on low for 1½ hours. Serve in warmed mugs.

SERVINGS:
10 MUGS

SPICY HOT CRANBERRY–LEMON PUNCH

Another cranberry concoction to serve at a fall feast, or even after a round of Halloween trick-or-treating.

2 cans (6 ounces each) frozen
    lemonade concentrate, slightly thawed
2 cups cranberry juice cocktail
½ teaspoon ground allspice
¼ teaspoon ground cinnamon
Pinch of salt
3 cups water
Cinnamon sticks, for garnish

Place the lemonade (undiluted), cranberry juice, spices, and water in a saucepan. Bring to a boil over medium heat, then lower the heat and simmer for 10 minutes. Serve piping hot in punch cups, with a bit of cinnamon stick for garnish.

SERVINGS: 12 PUNCH CUPS

HOT MOCHA PUNCH

Thanksgiving guests just might stay later for second helpings of pie. If they do, here is a perfect companion. No trouble at all to make— and very good.

1 quart chocolate ice cream
2 quarts hot coffee
Grated nutmeg, for garnish

Place the ice cream in a punch bowl. Pour the hot coffee over it, and beat the mixture with a wire whisk until the ice cream is nearly melted. Serve in punch cups with a dash of nutmeg for garnish.

SERVINGS: 16 PUNCH CUPS

WINTER WONDERFULS

Thirsty guests assembled by a warm fireside, shoppers chilled to the bone, carolers bundled for a night of song, wee ones helping to decorate the tree, festive open houses, and holiday dinner parties . . . something for everyone!

Although there are plenty of hot-drink suggestions here for warming a blustery winter night or greeting cold sledders and skiers, there are also a few icy surprises, like the lovely granités. They make light palate-pleasing starters at any festive occasion.

Nothing is more welcoming than a punch bowl full of frothy, creamy eggnog during this party season. Eggnog keeps well and is wonderful to have on hand in the refrigerator. Also, don't forget Valentine's Day and St. Patrick's Day—wintertime events that call for a special celebratory brew.

LEMON/TARRAGON GRANITÉ

A cross between a drinkable slush and a spoonable one, granités make refreshing appetizers—excellent with fish or poultry—as well as tasty between-course palate cleansers. For sweet granités, see pages 64 and 65.

2 cups water
1 cup fresh lemon juice
¼ cup sugar
1 teaspoon dried tarragon
1 teaspoon grated lemon zest
Few drops yellow food coloring
Fresh mint leaves, for garnish

1. Combine the water, lemon juice, sugar, and tarragon in a large saucepan and bring to a boil. Continue boiling until the quantity is reduced by half, 2 to 3 minutes.

2. Pour the liquid through a strainer into a cake pan. Mix in the grated lemon zest and the food coloring, and set aside to cool. When cool, place in the freezer and freeze uncovered until solid, about 2 hours.

3. Remove the pan from the freezer and scoop out the frozen granité with a spatula, dropping the chunks into a large mixing bowl. Beat with an electric mixer until slushy, and then spoon into a large covered plastic container and refreeze, about 1 hour.

4. To serve, soften slightly (30 minutes at room temperature; 30 seconds on high in a microwave) and scoop out portions. Serve in empty lemon shells, if desired, and decorate with mint leaves.

SERVINGS: 6 PUNCH CUPS

TOMATO GRANITÉ

Season this savory, icy drink with cilantro—an unusual start for a spirited holiday dinner party.

2 cups water
1 cup white vinegar
½ cup (packed) fresh cilantro leaves
1 can (14½ ounces) stewed tomatoes
Parsley sprigs, for garnish

1. Combine the water, vinegar, and cilantro in a large saucepan, and bring to a boil. Continue boiling until the quantity is reduced by half, 2 to 3 minutes.

2. Pour the reduced mixture through a strainer into a cake pan.

3. Pour the stewed tomatoes into a blender and blend on medium speed for 1 minute. Stir the tomatoes into the mixture in the cake pan. When cool, place in the freezer and freeze uncovered until solid, about 2 hours.

4. Remove the cake pan from the freezer, and scoop out the frozen granité with a spatula, dropping the chunks into a large mixing bowl. Beat with an electric mixer until slushy.

Spoon into a large covered plastic container and refreeze, about 1 hour.

5. To serve, soften slightly (30 minutes at room temperature; 30 seconds on high in a microwave) and scoop out portions. Serve in hollowed-out tomato halves, if desired, and garnish with parsley.

SERVINGS: 6 PUNCH CUPS

THE ONLY TOAST YOU NEED TO KNOW

"Let's drink to all the joy-filled hours
Grinning babes and dainty flowers
Forget the tears we may have shed
The jobs we've lost, the jerks we've wed.
Look to the stars, look to the sun
Here's to laughter and here's to fun!"

ASPARAGUS APPETIZER

Double the quantity for a delicious opener at a small buffet or for a ladies' luncheon. You can serve it hot or cold.

1 can (10½ ounces) condensed cream
   of asparagus soup
1 cup cold milk
¾ teaspoon onion salt
¾ teaspoon celery salt
Juice of ½ lemon
Salt and freshly ground black pepper,
   to taste
Paprika, for garnish

Combine all the ingredients, through the salt and pepper, in a blender and blend until smooth, 1 minute. Pour into pretty demitasse cups or crystal-clear punch cups, and give each a sprinkle of paprika.

SERVINGS: 4 SMALL CUPS

NONSHRIMP COCKTAIL

Finished with your holiday shopping? This is for you!

¾ cup tomato juice
1 teaspoon prepared
   horseradish
Dash of Tabasco sauce
Dash of Worcestershire
   sauce
Dash of lemon juice,
   preferably fresh
Salt and freshly ground black pepper,
   to taste
Twist of lemon zest, for garnish

Put all the ingredients, through the salt and pepper, in a short fat glass and stir briskly. Add some crushed ice and a lemon twist.

SERVINGS: 1 COCKTAIL GLASS

PINK ELEPHANT

These look attractive when served in large brandy snifters—a tasty way to toast the New Year.

1 teaspoon lime juice, preferably fresh
1 teaspoon grenadine syrup
1 teaspoon sugar
½ cup bitter lemon soda
½ cup pink grapefruit juice

1. Mix the lime juice, grenadine, and sugar together in a snifter.

2. Add ice cubes, the bitter lemon, and the grapefruit juice. Stir and serve.

SERVINGS: 1 BRANDY SNIFTER

GINGER MINT

A quick highball—extra good when served in a frosted glass.

1 lime
Ginger ale
Several sprigs of fresh mint, for garnish

Squeeze the lime juice into a tall frosted glass. Add some ice cubes, and fill with ginger ale. Stir, and add mint sprigs.

SERVINGS: 1 TALL GLASS

ROOSTER'S PET

Although commercial eggnog is available during the holiday season, it is easy to make your own and great to have some ready for unexpected guests—and you don't have to wait for the holidays!

3 cups cold milk
3 eggs (see Note, page 34)
3 tablespoons sugar
1 teaspoon vanilla
extract
Pinch of grated nutmeg
Grated nutmeg, for garnish

1. Place all the ingredients, through the pinch of nutmeg, in a blender and blend for 20 seconds.

2. Pour into a small serving bowl and sprinkle with nutmeg.

SERVINGS: 8 SMALL PUNCH CUPS

RED HOT GRANNY

Not such a fancy-schmancy appetizer—but easy to make and it inspires appetites for a hearty meal.

3 cans (10½ ounces each)
condensed beef broth
1½ cups water
2 teaspoons prepared horseradish
½ teaspoon minced dill weed,
preferably fresh
Lemon slivers or parsley sprigs,
for garnish

Combine all the ingredients, through the dill, in a medium-size saucepan and bring just to a boil. Reduce the heat and simmer briefly. Serve in small mugs or punch cups, with a sliver of lemon or a sprig of parsley for garnish.

SERVINGS: 8 SMALL CUPS

MOCK MOOSE MILK

A warm drink for a cold day. Fill a thermos for skaters, skiers, and sledders.

3 cups milk
3 tablespoons sugar
½ teaspoon almond extract
1 teaspoon rum flavoring

1. In a small heavy saucepan, heat the milk just until tiny bubbles form around the edge. Remove from heat.

2. Add the rest of the ingredients to the milk. Stir to blend well.

3. Serve immediately in heated mugs, or pour into a thermos to serve later on.

SERVINGS: *3 MUGS*

CARAMEL MILK

No more tossing and turning—this makes a sweet and soothing bedtime drink. Pleasant dreams are a sure thing.

1 cup hot milk
2 tablespoons dark brown sugar
Dash of vanilla extract

Combine all the ingredients in a mug. Stir, and serve warm.

SERVINGS: *1 MUG*

CARAMEL EGGNOG

A subtle crème brûlée flavor in a creamy eggnog drink.

⅓ cup sugar
1½ cups boiling water
3 very fresh eggs,
    separated (see
    Note, page 34)
Dash of vanilla
    extract
1 quart light cream or half-and-half
Pinch of salt
Maraschino cherries, for garnish

1. Place the sugar in a small saucepan over low heat and stir until it forms an amber liquid (caramel). Watch this carefully; it will take about 1 minute.

2. Slowly add the boiling water and stir until the caramel dissolves. Remove from the heat, pour into a small bowl, and chill.

3. Meanwhile, beat the egg yolks in a mixing bowl until they are thick. Set them aside.

4. Place the egg whites in a separate bowl, add the vanilla, and beat until they are very stiff and form peaks.

5. Just before serving, combine the caramel with the cream in a small punch bowl. Then gently fold the egg whites into the egg yolks. Carefully stir the eggs into the caramel-cream mixture, and add the salt.

6. Serve immediately, in punch cups or old-fashioned glasses, garnished with the cherries.

SERVINGS: 6 PUNCH CUPS

YULENOG

Good for caroling parties, when remembering the lyrics is important!

6 very fresh eggs, separated
  (see Note, page 34)
⅓ cup honey or sugar
5 cups cold milk
2 tablespoons rum extract
1 teaspoon vanilla extract
1 cup whipped cream
Grated nutmeg, for garnish

1. Beat the egg whites with an electric mixer until soft peaks form.

2. Add the egg yolks and the honey. Continue beating.

3. Slowly add the milk, then the rum and vanilla extracts, and beat until blended. Chill.

4. Just before serving, fold in the whipped cream and sprinkle with nutmeg.

SERVINGS: *12 PUNCH CUPS*

COFFEE EGGNOG

Coffee-flavored eggnog is a real treat, and this recipe is flavorful and simple to make.

1 quart commercial eggnog
1 quart strong coffee, chilled
½ cup sugar
Pinch of grated nutmeg
Grated nutmeg, for garnish

1. Place half of the eggnog, coffee, sugar, and nutmeg in a blender and blend for 30 seconds. Pour into a small punch bowl. Repeat with the other half and stir the batches together.

2. Garnish with grated nutmeg.

SERVINGS: *12 PUNCH CUPS*

Note: Another way to make a coffee eggnog is to simply add 6 tablespoons of powdered instant coffee to Rooster's Pet (page 108) and adjust the sugar to taste.

ORANGE NOG SUPREME

The most exciting and delicious of all the eggnogs—more trouble to concoct, but well worth the effort.

2 quarts orange juice,
*   preferably fresh*
½ cup fresh lemon juice
6 very fresh eggs
*   (see Note, page 34)*
¼ cup sugar
¼ teaspoon ground
*   cinnamon*
¼ teaspoon ground cloves
¼ teaspoon ground ginger
Pinch of grated nutmeg
1 quart vanilla ice cream
1 quart ginger ale, chilled
Grated nutmeg, for garnish

1. Place half of the ingredients, through the pinch of nutmeg, in a blender and blend on medium speed until smooth, 30 seconds. Pour into a large container. Repeat with the other half and combine the two batches. Cover and refrigerate.

2. Place the ice cream and ginger ale in a large punch bowl. Break up the ice cream into chunks. Then, using a whisk, beat the mixture until it is well blended.

3. Add the refrigerated ingredients and continue beating until all are incorporated.

4. Sprinkle with nutmeg and serve.

SERVINGS: 24 PUNCH CUPS

BANANA EGGNOG

An energy-filled drink for folk who are tired after a New Year's Eve bash.

3 very fresh eggs (see Note, page 34)
3 bananas, cut into small pieces
½ pint vanilla ice cream, softened
3½ cups cold milk
Pinch of grated nutmeg
Grated nutmeg, for garnish

1. Place the eggs, bananas, ice cream, 1½ cups of the milk, and pinch of nutmeg in a blender. Blend on high speed until creamy, 30 seconds.

2. Pour the mixture into a small punch bowl and stir in the remaining milk.

3. Sprinkle with grated nutmeg and serve in punch cups.

SERVINGS: 6 PUNCH CUPS

COFFEE PUNCH

For a glorious open house—very easy to make and very easy to drink.

4 quarts strong coffee,
   chilled
1 quart light cream
   or half-and-half
1 tablespoon vanilla extract
1 quart vanilla ice cream, softened
1 cup sugar
Whipped cream and shaved chocolate,
   for garnish

1. Combine the coffee, cream, and vanilla in a large bowl.

2. Place the ice cream in a large punch bowl and slowly pour the coffee mixture over it. Stir to blend with a wire whisk, adding the sugar gradually.

3. To serve, ladle the punch into cups and top each with a dollop of whipped cream and a sprinkling of chocolate.

SERVINGS: 32 PUNCH CUPS

CANDLELIGHT HOLLY–DAY PUNCH

Hot or cold, this punch tastes best when served by candlelight. For the cold version, make an ice ring with holly leaves (no berries, please) and fresh cranberries.

> 2 quarts apple cider
> 1 quart orange juice, preferably fresh
> Juice of 2 lemons
> 4 cinnamon sticks (3 inches each)
> 2 tablespoons whole cloves
> 1 tablespoon ground allspice
> Pinch of grated nutmeg
> Pinch of ground mace
> 1 cup honey

COLD: Combine all the ingredients in a large saucepan, stir, and bring to a boil. Reduce the heat and simmer for 10 minutes. Strain the punch into several large pitchers and refrigerate. At serving time, pour into a large punch bowl and add the holly ice ring.

HOT: Combine all the ingredients in a large saucepan, stir, and bring to a boil. Reduce the heat and simmer for 10 minutes. Strain into a prewarmed punch bowl and serve immediately.

SERVINGS: 20 PUNCH CUPS

THE DRY EDITH

Try this or the Red Nun if your stomach feels bloated after a festive holiday party.

1 large glass club soda (with ice)
Large dash of bitters (see Note, page 36)
1 piece lemon zest
    Add the bitters to the iced club soda, drop in a healthy chunk of lemon zest, and stir.

SERVINGS: 1 TALL GLASS

RED NUN

1 large glass 7-Up (with ice)
Dash of bitters
Stir the bitters into the 7-Up, and down the hatch.

SERVINGS: 1 TALL GLASS

HANUKKAH PUNCH

A fast punch for 30 that goes especially well with those Hanukkah fruits, cookies, and candies.

1 can (6 ounces) frozen lemonade
concentrate, thawed
1 can (6 ounces) frozen orange juice
concentrate, thawed
6 cups water
½ cup grenadine syrup
1 quart ginger ale, chilled
Wafer-thin lemon slices for garnish

Combine the juices, water, and grenadine in a punch bowl. Just before serving, add some ice cubes and gently stir in the ginger ale. Put a lemon slice and a cherry in each punch cup, and serve.

SERVINGS: 18 TO 20 PUNCH CUPS

CRIMSON CHRISTMAS PUNCH

This delectable holiday punch speaks for itself—rich in color and easy to make. The trick for elegance lies in the serving.

1 quart cranberry juice cocktail
1 quart red currant juice (see Note)
1 quart 7-Up chilled
Ice ring made with lime slices and cherries
(see page 2)

Combine the fruit juices in a punch bowl. Just before serving, stir in the 7-Up and add the ice ring.

SERVINGS: 20 PUNCH CUPS

Note: Red currant juice is available in larger supermarkets and specialty food stores.

MOCHA MIA

Easy and delicious for an intimate moment by the fireside . . .

1 square (1 ounce) unsweetened chocolate,
    coarsely chopped
¼ cup boiling water
1 tablespoon powdered instant coffee
1 tablespoon sugar
1½ cups cold milk
Whipped cream and chocolate shavings,
    for garnish

1. Place all the ingredients, through the milk, in a blender and blend on high speed for 20 seconds.

2. Pour into 2 tall glasses, and top with a dollop of whipped cream and some chocolate shavings.

SERVINGS: 2 TALL GLASSES

CHOCOLATE ESPRESSO

Here's an opportunity to use those delicate demitasse cups. The zest in the whipped cream plays off the deep mocha flavor beautifully.

½ cup heavy (whipping) cream
1 tablespoon sugar
Dash of vanilla extract
½ teaspoon grated orange zest
¼ cup powdered instant espresso coffee
1 cup strong hot chocolate
1 cup boiling water
Grated nutmeg, for garnish

1. Using an electric mixer, whip the cream together with the sugar and vanilla until soft peaks form. Fold in the orange zest. Set aside.

2. Combine the instant espresso, hot chocolate, and boiling water in a glass or ceramic coffeepot and stir.

3. Pour the coffee into demitasse cups, and top each one with a spoonful of the whipped cream. Garnish with a sprinkling of nutmeg.

SERVINGS: 6 DEMITASSE CUPS

QUICK MOCHA–CAPPUCCINO

This is excellent as an after-dinner drink, as well as a warm welcome home for winter athletes.

> 2 envelopes (2 ounces each) cocoa mix
> 3 heaping tablespoons powdered instant coffee
> 1 cup heavy (whipping) cream, heated but not boiling
> Pinch of ground cinnamon
> 3 cups boiling water
> Ground cinnamon, for garnish

1. Place the cocoa, coffee, hot cream, and pinch of cinnamon in a blender and blend until frothy.

2. Fill coffee cups two-thirds full with the boiling water, and add the hot mocha froth. Stir, and sprinkle with extra cinnamon.

SERVINGS: 8 COFFEE CUPS

FESTIVE MOCHA

Festivities can begin or end with a pretty glass filled with unusually delicious chilled coffee.

> 3 cups strong coffee, chilled
> 1 pint coffee ice cream
> Dash of vanilla extract
> ¼ cup chocolate syrup

Place all the ingredients in a blender and blend on medium speed until smooth, 1 minute. Serve in fancy goblets.

SERVINGS: 4 GOBLETS

FRENCH CHOCOLATE

Now this is a great cup of hot chocolate! It will surely fuel up the tree trimmers. And remember to leave a cup for Santa!

½ cup heavy (whipping) cream
3 squares (3 ounces) unsweetened
    chocolate
¾ cup water
¾ cup sugar
Pinch of salt
1 quart milk, heated but not boiling
Whipped cream and chocolate shavings,
    for garnish

1. Using an electric mixer, whip the cream until soft peaks form. Set aside.

2. Combine the chocolate and the water in a small saucepan. Cook over low heat, stirring constantly, until the chocolate is melted, about 5 minutes.

3. Add the sugar and salt, and boil gently for 3 minutes, stirring constantly.

4. Remove from the heat and fold in the whipped cream.

5. Put 1 tablespoon of this chocolate mixture in each cup, add hot milk to fill, and stir. Top with a spoonful of whipped cream and some chocolate shavings.

SERVINGS: 6 COFFEE CUPS

DECORATING WITH CHOCOLATE

To grate chocolate: Chill a square of baking chocolate first, then put it through a hand grinder. You can use a cheese grater, but be sure to go slowly to prevent knuckle scrapes.

For decorative curls: Bring the chocolate to room temperature. Shave off thin strips with a paring knife or a vegetable peeler.

CHOCOLATE SIN

Warm and wonderful—hot chocolate for two goes well with an intense game of backgammon.

*1 square (1 ounce) unsweetened
   chocolate
¼ cup sugar
Dash of vanilla extract
Pinch of ground cinnamon
Pinch of salt
3 cups milk
Mini marshmallows, for garnish*

1. Carefully melt the chocolate in a heavy saucepan over very low heat, or in the top of a double boiler over simmering water.

2. Add the spices and the milk, and stir to mix well. Heat until very hot but not boiling. Serve with a dollop of whipped cream, or float some marshmallows on top.

SERVINGS: 2 MUGS

CHOCOLATE WHIPPED CREAM

Regular hot coffee—prepared by any method—becomes doubly delicious when topped with chocolate whipped cream.

*1 pint heavy (whipping) cream
3 heaping tablespoons powdered cocoa mix
3 heaping tablespoons sugar
½ teaspoon vanilla extract*

Combine all the ingredients in a bowl and whip with an electric mixer until the cream forms peaks.

SERVINGS: 4

AUNT FANNY'S PARTY PUNCH

This punch is proportioned for fifty. It is an open house *must*.

> 1 large can (46 ounces)
>   pineapple juice
> 1 large can (46 ounces) apricot nectar
> 1 quart orange juice, preferably fresh
> 2 quarts orange sherbet, slightly softened
> 1 quart vanilla ice cream, slightly softened
> 1 package (10 ounces) frozen strawberries,
>   thawed and drained
> 2 quarts ginger ale, chilled
> Pineapple cubes, mint sprigs, and whole
>   strawberries, for garnish

Combine all the fruit juices in a large punch bowl. Beat the sherbet and ice cream in with a whisk, leaving them in small chunks. Add the strawberries. Gently stir in the ginger ale, and place a large piece of ice or an ice ring in the bowl. Add enough pineapple, mint, and strawberry garnish so that your guests will scoop up a bit with each serving.

SERVINGS: 50 PUNCH CUPS

ESKIMO PUNCH

A coldy but goody. Create a decorative garnish for these by alternating pineapple cubes and maraschino cherries on a toothpick and serving one with each cup.

> 3 cups apricot nectar
> 3 cups pineapple juice
> 1 quart orange juice, preferably fresh
> 1 quart 7-Up
> 1 quart ginger ale or club soda, chilled
> Pineapple cubes and maraschino cherries,
>   for garnish

Combine all the juices in a punch bowl and stir. Add some ice cubes, and gently mix in the 7-Up and ginger ale. Serve with fruit kabob garnishes.

SERVINGS: 28 PUNCH CUPS

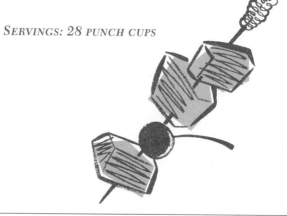

GRAPE FRAPPE

A drink rich in color and flavor makes a welcome change at a small winter get-together.

> 2 cups grape juice
> 2 tablespoons fresh lemon juice
> ½ cup sugar
> 2 cups water
> 2 cups light cream or half-and-half
> 1 pint grape ice cream or sherbet
> Wafer-thin lemon slices, for garnish

1. Place the grape juice, lemon juice, and sugar in a large pitcher and stir.

2. Gradually add the water and cream, stirring with each addition.

3. Put half of the mixture in a blender and add the ice cream. Blend on medium speed until smooth, 1 minute.

4. Return the blender mixture to the pitcher and stir well.

5. Serve in tall glasses over cracked ice. Garnish each serving with a lemon slice.

SERVINGS: 8 TALL GLASSES

PURPLE PASSION

This is a delicious and inexpensive way to serve the multitudes—those thirsty dancers at a winter wedding, for instance.

> 4 quarts grape
>   juice
> 1 quart lemon juice (can
>   be made from concentrate)
> 1 quart pineapple juice
> 9 quarts club soda, chilled
> 4 cups sugar, dissolved in 2 cups
>   hot water
> Maraschino cherries, for garnish

1. Place a large ice ring in a clean metal washtub or other large container.

2. Add the rest of the ingredients to the tub, and stir gently to mix.

3. Place a maraschino cherry in the bottom of each punch cup, and serve.

SERVINGS: 100 PUNCH CUPS

HOT SPICED GRAPE JUICE

This can be made ahead and kept on hand in your crockpot as a welcoming hot drink for New Year's Eve guests.

1 quart grape juice
1 quart cranberry juice cocktail
4 whole cloves
1 large stick cinnamon (5 inches)
3 whole allspice
½ cup (packed) dark brown sugar
⅓ cup granulated sugar

1. Place all the ingredients in a large saucepan and stir until they are well mixed.

2. Cook over low heat until the sugar is dissolved, about 10 minutes.

3. Strain, and serve in mugs.

SERVINGS: 10 MUGS

STUPID CUPID

A fabulous drink for an after-school Valentine's Day party.

2 cups frozen
*   strawberries, thawed*
*   and crushed*
1 cup orange juice,
*   preferably fresh*
⅓ cup lemon juice,
*   preferably fresh*
1 quart cold milk
Maraschino cherries,
*   for garnish*

1. Place all the ingredients, through the milk, in a blender and blend on medium speed for 1 minute.

2. Pour the mixture into a pitcher, cover, and refrigerate until well chilled.

3. Serve in frosted glasses, topped with a cherry.

SERVINGS: 6 TALL GLASSES

SWEETHEART BERRY-BERRY

Enough for a couple of romantics enjoying a Valentine's Day brunch.

1 pint raspberry sherbet
2 cups cold milk

Place the ingredients in a blender and blend on high speed for 15 seconds. Serve in tall glasses.

SERVINGS: 2 TALL GLASSES

SWEET SUE

This drink will slip down along with chips and dips and midnight sandwiches at a late night Valentine's Day get-together.

1 quart cranberry juice cocktail
1 quart 7-Up
Juice of 1 lime
½ cup sugar
Wafer-thin lime slices, for garnish

1. Place all the ingredients, through the sugar, in a large pitcher and stir until they are well mixed.

2. Serve over ice in tall glasses, and garnish each with a lime slice.

SERVINGS: 8 TALL GLASSES

SHILLELAGH SIP

Prepare this fizzy, festive potable for a St. Patrick's Day party.

1 jar (8 ounces) green maraschino
cherries
2 quarts limeade, made from concentrate
1 quart lemon-lime soda, chilled

1. Make an ice ring using the green maraschino cherry liquid, cherries, and water (see page 2). Keep in the freezer until ready.

2. Place the limeade and lemon-lime soda in a punch bowl that is large enough to hold the punch plus the ice ring. Stir.

3. Immediately before serving, carefully place the ice ring in the punch bowl.

SERVINGS: 20 PUNCH CUPS

LIME TIME

Something cool and green for St. Patrick's Day. Good for adults and children alike.

2 quarts pineapple juice
1 cup sugar syrup (see page 69)
1 quart lemon-lime soda, chilled
1 quart lime sherbet, softened
Green maraschino cherries or wafer-thin
lime slices, for garnish

1. Place a large cake of ice in a large punch bowl. Then add the pineapple juice and the sugar syrup. Stir gently to blend well.

2. Add the lemon-lime soda and the sherbet. Slowly stir the sherbet into the punch with a whisk, and blend well.

3. Garnish the punch bowl with cherries or lime slices, and serve.

SERVINGS: 20 PUNCH CUPS

DRINKS FOR ALL OCCASIONS

CONVERSION TABLE

OVEN TEMPERATURES

FAHRENHEIT	GAS MARK	CELSIUS
250	½	120
275	1	140
300	2	150
325	3	160
350	4	180
375	5	190
400	6	200
425	7	220
450	8	230
475	9	240
500	10	260

Note: Reduce the temperature by 20°C (68°F) for fan-assisted ovens.

APPROXIMATE EQUIVALENTS

1 stick butter = 8 TBS = 4 OZ = ½ CUP

1 CUP all-purpose presifted flour or
    dried bread crumbs = 5 OZ

1 CUP granulated sugar = 8 OZ

1 CUP (packed) brown sugar = 6 OZ

1 CUP confectioners' sugar = 4 ½ OZ

1 CUP honey/syrup = 11 OZ

1 CUP grated cheese = 4 OZ

1 CUP dried beans = 6 OZ

1 large egg = 2 oz = about ¼ CUP

1 egg yoke = about 1 TBS

1 egg white = about 2 TBS

Note: All the conversions shown here are approximate but close enough to be useful when converting from one system to another.

LIQUID CONVERSIONS

US	IMPERIAL	METRIC
2 TBS	1 FL OZ	30 ML
3 TBS	1 ½ FL OZ	45 ML
¼ CUP	2 FL OZ	60 ML
⅓ CUP	2 ½ FL OZ	75 ML
⅓ CUP + 1 TBS	3 FL OZ	90 ML
⅓ CUP + 2 TBS	3 ½ FL OZ	100 ML
½ CUP	4 FL OZ	125 ML
⅔ CUP	5 FL OZ	150 ML
¾ CUP	6 FL OZ	175 ML
¾ CUP + 2 TBS	7 FL OZ	200 ML
1 CUP	8 FL OZ	250 ML
1 CUP + 2 TBS	9 FL OZ	275 ML
1 ¼ CUPS	10 FL OZ	300 ML
1 ⅓ CUPS	11 FL OZ	325 ML
1 ½ CUPS	12 FL OZ	350 ML
1 ⅔ CUPS	13 FL OZ	375 ML
1 ¾ CUPS	14 FL OZ	400 ML
1 ¾ CUPS + 2 TBS	15 FL OZ	450 ML
1 PINT (2 CUPS)	16 FL OZ	500 ML
2 ½ CUPS	1 PINT	600 ML
3 ¾ CUPS	1 ½ PINTS	900 ML
4 CUPS	1 ¾ PINTS	1 LITER

WEIGHT CONVERSIONS

US/UK	METRIC	US/UK	METRIC
½ OZ	15 G	7 OZ	200 G
1 OZ	30 G	8 OZ	250 G
1 ½ OZ	45 G	9 OZ	275 G
2 OZ	60 G	10 OZ	300 G
2 ½ OZ	75 G	11 OZ	325 G
3 OZ	90 G	12 OZ	350 G
3 ½ OZ	100 G	13 OZ	375 G
4 OZ	125 G	14 OZ	400 G
5 OZ	150 G	15 OZ	450 G
6 OZ	175 G	1 LB	500 G

INDEX